BEAUTIFUL WORD™ BIBLE STUDIES

John
Believe I Am

STUDY GUIDE + STREAMING VIDEO

EIGHT SESSIONS

MEGAN FATE MARSHMAN

HarperChristian Resources

John Study Guide
© 2022 by Megan Fate Marshman

Requests for information should be addressed to:
HarperChristian Resources, 3900 Sparks Dr. SE, Grand Rapids, Michigan 49546

ISBN 978–0–310–15265-1 (softcover)
ISBN 978–0–310–15266-8 (ebook)

HarperChristian Resources titles may be purchased in bulk for church, business, fundraising, or ministry use. For information, please e-mail ResourceSpecialist@ ChurchSource.com.

First Printing September 2022 / Printed in the United States of America

CONTENTS

WELCOME

Beautiful
WORD™
BIBLE STUDIES

John

Believe I Am

SOMETIMES the Bible can seem overwhelming. Where do you go for words of comfort when you're feeling overwhelmed, lost, or frustrated in life? What book of the Bible do you turn to for wisdom about the situations in which you find yourself?

The *Beautiful Word Bible Studies* series makes the Bible come alive in such a way that you know where to turn no matter where you find yourself on your spiritual journey.

The Gospel of John, the fourth account of the life of Jesus, is often regarded as one of the most beloved books of the Bible. Written by the disciple John, the writing is chock-full of insights and stories about Jesus that don't appear in the other three gospels. John brings an artistic vibe as he pens the details of the teachings, miracles, and resurrection of Jesus.

John reveals his heart behind his writing: "But these are written that you may believe that Jesus is the Messiah, the Son of God, and that by believing you may have life in his name" (John 20:31). This passionate Christ-follower wants everyone to know Jesus—whom He is, the depths of His power, and beauty and might.

The upcoming sessions explore the seven "I Am" statements of Jesus, which reveal the heart and presence of God with remarkable precision. The teaching plunges deep into what the Son of God meant when He identified Himself as the Bread of Life; the Light of the World; the Gate; the Good Shepherd; the Resurrection and the Life; the Way, the Truth, and the Life; and the Vine.

By diving into this beautiful book, you're invited to let the Holy Spirit lead you into more intimate understanding, adoration, and prayer as we experience life in His name together.

John reveals his heart behind his writing: "But these are written that you may believe that Jesus is the Messiah, the Son of God, and that by believing you may have life in his name" (John 20:31). This passionate Christ-follower wants everyone to know Jesus—whom He is, the depths of His power, and beauty and might.

HOW TO USE THIS GUIDE

GROUP INFORMATION AND SIZE RECOMMENDATIONS

The Beautiful Word *John* video study is designed to be experienced in a group setting such as a Bible study, small group, or other Sunday school class. After opening with a short activity, you will watch each video session and participate in a time of group discussion and reflection on what you're learning both from the video teaching and the personal Bible study between meetings. This content is rich and takes you through the entire gospel, so be prepared for a full experience of the depth of Scripture.

If you have a larger group (more than twelve people), consider breaking up into smaller groups during the discussion time. It is important that members of the group have the opportunities to ask questions, share ideas and experiences, as well as feel heard and seen—no matter their backgrounds and circumstances.

MATERIALS NEEDED AND LEADING A GROUP

Each participant should have his or her own study guide. Each study guide comes with an individual streaming video access code on the inside front cover. Every member of your group has full access to watch videos from the convenience of their chosen devices at any time—for missed group meetings, for rewatching, for sharing teaching with others, or if your group is short on meeting time and watching videos individually and then meeting makes the group experience doable and more realistic. We have worked very hard to make gathering around and studying the Word of God accessible and simple.

This study guide includes video outline notes, group discussion questions, a personal Bible study section for between group meetings, Beautiful Word coloring pages, and Scripture memory cards to deepen learning between sessions. Additionally, the leader will need to show the videos either by digital stream/download or on DVD. Streaming video access is included with each study guide.

There is a Leader's Guide in the back of this study guide so anyone can lead a group through this study. A lot of thought has been put into making the *Beautiful Word Bible Studies* series available to all—which included making it easy to lead, no matter your experience or acumen!

TIMING

The timing notations—for example, 20 minutes—indicate the lengths of the video segments and the suggested times for each activity or discussion. Within your allotted group meeting time, you may not get to all the discussion questions. Remember that the *quantity* of questions addressed isn't as important as the *quality* of the discussion.

Using the Leader's Guide in the back of the guide to review the content overview of each session and the group discussion questions in advance will give you a good idea of which questions you want to focus on as a leader or group facilitator.

FACILITATION

Each group should appoint a facilitator who is responsible for starting the video and keeping track of time during the activities and discussion. Facilitators may also read questions aloud, monitor discussions, prompt participants to respond, and ensure that everyone has opportunities to participate.

OPENING GROUP ACTIVITY

Depending on the amount of time you have to meet and the resources available, you'll want to begin the session with the group activity. You will find these activities on the group page that begins each session. The interactive icebreaker is designed to be a catalyst for group engagement and help participants prepare and transition to the ideas explored in the video teaching.

The leader or facilitator will want to read ahead to the following week's activity to see what will be needed and how participants may be able to contribute by bringing supplies or refreshments.

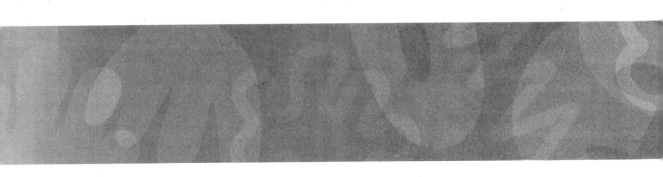

SESSION 1

BELIEVE
I AM

John

opening group activity [10-15 MINUTES]

WHAT YOU'LL NEED:

One sheet of blank paper for each person

Pens, markers, and/or watercolors

1. Use the paper and drawing/writing tools to write the words "I Am" on the top of the page. Then consider the seven *I Am* statements of Christ: the Bread of Life; the Light of the World; the Gate; the Good Shepherd; the Resurrection and the Life; the Way, the Truth, and the Life; and the Vine. Select the one that is most intriguing to you and draw a picture or write a description of that rich imagery on the sheet of paper.

I AM
the Bread of Life
the Light of the World
the Gate
the Good Shepherd
the Resurrection and the Life
the Way, the Truth, and the Life
the Vine

I AM THE VINE

2. Share your images or word pictures with each other as you discuss the following questions:

Which *I Am* statement is most intriguing to you?

Why did you select this image to draw or describe? Are there any details about what you created that are particularly important?

What do you hope to get out of this study?

watch session one video [21 MINUTES]

Leader, play the streaming video or DVD.

As you watch, take notes while thinking through:

What caught your attention?
What surprised you?
What made you reflect?

❊ Knowing *about* someone is the first step toward *really* knowing them.

❊ You're loved, so much so, you don't have to search for it anywhere else.

❊ If you want to know who the true God is, who exists eternally, look at Jesus, the Son.

❊ When you know someone's name, they become approachable.

❊ Signs always point to the purpose, the destination.

❊ Jesus is not a vending machine or projection of our desires.

SCRIPTURE covered in this session:
John 1:1–5, 14

group discussion questions [30-45 MINUTES]

"We're not just meant to know a lot about God. We can get to know Him personally. Knowing about someone is just the first step toward really knowing them. Thankfully, God has made Himself known to us through His Word and through His son, Christ Jesus."
—Megan

1. **Read** the phrases below and then place a star ☆ by the one that best describes you now and a circle ⬭ around the one that best describes spiritually where you'd like to be. Discuss why you made the selections.

   I've heard of God.

   I know some about God.

   I'm confused by God.

   I have lots of questions about God.

   I sometimes struggle to see the connection between Jesus and God.

   I know a good amount of truth about God but don't know how to spend time with Him.

   I know lots about God but don't experience the benefits of a relationship with Him.

   I feel like I deeply know God, and still want to know more of the fullness of God through Jesus.

2. **Read John 20:31 aloud to the group.** Megan highlights John's purpose when she gives an overview of the gospel. What are John's goals for you as a reader? What do you think it means for you to "have life in His name"? Share a time when you've experienced "life in His name."

3. **Read John 1:1–5 aloud or select a volunteer to read to the group.** What does this passage reveal about Jesus? What's most comforting to you? What's most challenging to you?

4. **Select two volunteers to read John 1:14 and Colossians 1:15 aloud to the group.** Ask the following questions regarding the passages:

   Why did God become flesh to dwell among us?

   What do you think God was trying to communicate about Himself in becoming flesh and dwelling among us?

   What does it say about God that He chose to communicate with us at all?

   What would the alternative look like? What are the ways that God communicates to us?

> "Why do we give someone or something a name? It is to identify, to distinguish, to characterize, to describe, to familiarize—but in a sense, it is also to contain, constrain, and even tame. When I know someone's name, they become approachable. They no longer need to be held at arm's length." —Megan

YOU'RE LOVED, SO MUCH SO, YOU DON'T HAVE TO SEARCH FOR IT ANYWHERE ELSE.

Go around the group answering a selection of the following questions:

On a scale of one to ten, how often do you go out of your way to find out someone's name?

How does knowing someone's name change your level of connection with the person?

What do you normally call God when you speak to Him?

How does this affect your level of connection with God?

In what areas of your life have you been tempted to hold God at arm's length?

And how might learning more about the names God calls Himself draw you closer to Him?

5. Imagine Jesus boldly declaring each *I Am* statement to you. Which of these do you most need to hear and experience today? Why? What steps can you take to become more aware of Jesus in this way?

"I am the bread of life" (John 6).
Just after feeding thousands.

"I am the light of the world" (John 8).
Jesus explaining the difference between true and false leaders.

"I am the gate for the sheep" (John 10).
"I am the good shepherd" (John 10).
Jesus clarifies His sacrificial love for His sheep.

"I am the resurrection and the life" (John 11).
Before raising Lazarus from the dead.

"I am the way and the truth and the life" (John 14).
Explaining the path to heaven.

"I am the true vine" (John 15).
Illustrating abiding.

*L*et's turn our lives toward Jesus, believe Him, and find life in His name.

close in prayer

Consider the following prompts as you pray together for:

- Opportunities to move from knowing *about* God to *really* knowing God

- Stronger, more vibrant belief in Jesus

- Personal encounters with the fullness of life through His name

preparation

To prepare for the next group session:

1. **Read John 1–6.**

2. Tackle the three days of the Session One Personal Study.

3. Memorize this week's passage using the Beautiful Word Scripture memory coloring page. As a bonus, look up the Scripture memory passage in different translations and take note of the variations.

4. If you've agreed to bring something for the next session's Opening Group Activity, get it ready.

IF YOU WANT TO KNOW WHO THE TRUE GOD IS, WHO EXISTS ETERNALLY, LOOK AT JESUS, THE SON.

"But these are written that you may believe that Jesus is the Messiah, the Son of God, and that by believing you may have life in his name."
—John 20:31

PERSONAL
STUDY TIME

DIGGING INTO THE

Beautiful
WORD™
BIBLE STUDIES

John

BELIEVE I AM

IN GREEK,
THE "WORD" (V. 1) IS
LOGOS, PRONOUNCED
(LAW-GAWS). LOGOS
IS THE POWER AND
PURPOSE OF HUMAN
LIFE. WHILE IT WAS
USUALLY ASSOCIATED
WITH IMPERSONAL
AND ABSTRACT FORCES
IN THE WORLD, JOHN
INTRODUCES HIS BOOK
BY SAYING THAT THE
POWER AND PURPOSE
AND MEANING FOR
LIFE'S EXISTENCE
IS NOT AN ABSTRACT
PRINCIPLE, IT'S A
PERSON—JESUS.

DAY 1
John 1-2

Like Matthew and Luke, John offers a rich genealogy, but unlike the other gospels, his genealogy goes back before time began. John's opening words parallel those of Genesis 1:1, "in the beginning." This is a genealogy of eternity, of the pre-existent One. We often consider eternity in terms of moving forward, but Genesis and John hint toward eternity in the past, and a God who existed before the beginning.

1. **Read John 1:1–5.** What characteristics of God the Father's relationship with His son, Jesus, does John reveal right away? How is each one significant to you?

The Apostle John quickly introduces another man by the name of John, who is often known as John the Baptist.

2. **Read John 1:6–18** and fill in the chart below. What stands out to you most about the characteristics and mission of John the Baptist? Of Jesus Christ?

READ	OBSERVE	DESCRIBE
John 1:6–8, 15	Characteristics and Mission of John the Baptist	
John 1:9–14, 16–18	Characteristics and Mission of Jesus Christ	

3. **Read John 1:19–34.** How does John the Baptist stay on mission when it comes to proclaiming Christ?

What empowers you to stay on mission when it comes to sharing the good news of Jesus?

What tends to distract you or pull you away?

JOHN'S OPENING WORDS PARALLEL THOSE OF **Genesis 1:1,** "IN THE BEGINNING."

4. **Read John 1:35–50.** What stands out to you about the loving way Jesus meets each about-to-be disciple right where they were? Fill in the chart below.

ABOUT-TO-BE DISCIPLES	WHAT STANDS OUT TO YOU ABOUT THE WAY JESUS LOVINGLY MEETS THEM?
John the Baptist's Disciples	
Andrew and Simon	
Philip	
Nathanael	

Why do you think Jesus doesn't take the same approach for each person?

What are some of the unique ways in which Jesus has met you and revealed His love?

The first miracle Jesus performs in John's Gospel takes place at a wedding in Cana.

5. **Read John 2:1–12.** Why do you think Jesus' mother trusts Him so much?

On the continuum below, how persistent are you in prayerfully asking something from Jesus. Do you think persistence in prayer changes God or changes you? Explain.

❶←❷–❸–❹–❺–❻–❼–❽–❾→❿

I may ask once or twice and then I let it go.   I'm dogged in determination.

6. **Read John 2:13–25.** Make a list of Jesus' actions in the temple. Circle the action that may have been the most startling to those in the temple.

- _____
- _____
- _____
- _____
- _____

OFTEN THROUGHOUT THE BIBLE WHENEVER GOD IS DOING SOMETHING NEW AND SIGNIFICANT, HIS WORK IS COUPLED WITH A MIRACLE. ONCE JESUS CALLS THE DISCIPLES, HE PERFORMS HIS FIRST MIRACLE, OR SIGN, BY TURNING WATER INTO WINE. THE MIRACLES OF JESUS WILL INCREASE IN POWER, SCOPE, AND SIGNIFICANCE THE FURTHER YOU READ.

What compelled Jesus to be so radical in His response?

What is righteous anger and how does Jesus model this for us?

Take a moment to open your heart to the Holy Spirit. Ask if there are any areas in your life He wants to clean up, make right, or overturn to make you more like Jesus. As you consider your life and what you've noticed about yourself lately, how do you think the Holy Spirit's intercessory prayers on your behalf are being answered in your awareness?

Remember, God is with you on the journey toward being spiritually formed into the likeness of Christ. Making you more aware of yourself might be one way He is drawing you to Himself to transform your life through *His* power and not merely your effort. Write your response below.

7. How might what you've written above be holding you back from experiencing the fullness of life "in His name" (John 20:31)? What can you do about it?

DAY 2
John 3–4

Throughout John's Gospel, Jesus readily responds to the spiritually curious. In chapters 3 and 4, the message of salvation is delivered to three very different kinds of people. The first is a Pharisee, by the name of Nicodemus. Because of his religious stature in the community, he approaches Jesus in the night when no one will recognize him.

1. **Read John 3:1–21.** What spiritual inquiries and questions does Nicodemus pose to Jesus?

   What do you think motivates Nicodemus to pursue Jesus?

   What one spiritual question are you really wrestling with right now?

   What's preventing you from exploring that question on your own through prayer and alongside others with loving, faith-filled friends?

2. What does Jesus reveal about Himself in His response to Nicodemus? (Hint: John 3:16)

"THE **WIND** BLOWS WHEREVER IT PLEASES. YOU HEAR ITS SOUND, BUT YOU CANNOT TELL WHERE IT COMES FROM OR WHERE IT IS GOING. SO IT IS WITH EVERYONE BORN OF THE **SPIRIT**."

—JOHN 3:8

Although we can not see the wind, we can see and experience the effects of the wind. The same is true of the Holy Spirit. While we cannot see Him, we can be confident He is always moving. Our task is not to control Him but to open our hearts to whatever He is already doing in and through us.

Practically, in addition to asking, "God what should I do?" we can also ask, "Holy Spirit, what are you already doing?" From there, we can open ourselves to the ways the Holy Spirit might be wanting to use all things to form us more into the likeness of Jesus (Romans 8:26–29).

What hope and challenges do you find in verses 16–21? Fill in the chart below.

READ	PERSONAL HOPE	PERSONAL CHALLENGE
John 3:16–21		

The opening chapters of John cover crucial encounters at breakneck speed: the miracle at Cana, the cleansing of the Temple, the questions of Nicodemus. Then, the text circles back to John the Baptist and one of his last testimonies before his death.

3. **Read John 3:22–36.** What does John the Baptist say about Jesus?

How does this echo what Jesus says about Himself in John 3:11–21?

What parallels do you see between John 3:16 and John 3:36? What additional terms does verse 36 add? What is the connection between *believe* and *obey*?

Do you wholly, deeply believe that in Jesus Christ you experience everlasting life with God? How does obedience reveal the sincerity of belief (v. 36)?

What prevents you from believing more deeply?

To the Jewish, the Samaritans were villains, a despised, second-rate people. The hostility was so bad in the first centuries, devout Jews would walk many miles to avoid stepping on their despised land. Rather than avoiding the territory, Jesus made a beeline toward the Samaritan people and one particular woman.

While Nicodemus approaches Jesus at night for fear of what people thought, now Jesus approaches someone He shouldn't be seen with in broad daylight. But like Nicodemus, this woman is hiding, too. She's got a checkered past, and she knows the safest time for her to go to the watering hole is during the heat of the day when the fewest people will be around.

4. **Read John 4:1–9.** Circle ◯ the words below that best describe Jesus' response to the woman at the well.

Snooty	Kind	Graceful	Judging
Cruel	Rude	Patient	Compassionate
Demanding	Welcoming	Loving	Peaceful

How do you think the woman expected to be treated?

Describe the last time you were disarmed by someone's kindness and love.

SAMARIA WAS THE CAPITAL OF THE **NORTHERN KINGDOM OF ISRAEL.** OVER THE CENTURIES, HOSTILITY ERUPTED TOWARD THOSE IN THE REGION. THEY DESIRED TO **WORSHIP IN SHECHEM** RATHER THAN **JERUSALEM** AND AFTER **INTERMARRYING** WITH FOREIGNERS, THE JEWISH PEOPLE ACCUSED THEM OF IDOLATRY AND STRAYING FROM GOD.

Describe the last time you disarmed someone by kindness and love.

What prevents you from doing this more often?

5. **Read John 4:10–26.** How does Jesus tenderly expose and respond to the shame in the woman's life? (Hint: vv. 16–17)

Do you think Jesus exposes and responds to the shame in your life as tenderly as He does to this woman? Why or why not?

What does Jesus reveal about Himself in this passage?

To worship God in spirit and in truth is to worship the Father, through the Son, by the power of the Holy Spirit. Worship is a response to the truth of all that God is with all that we are. True worship is a response that is initiated by the work of the Spirit in our hearts to the truth about whom God is or what He has done—in and through His Son.

What does it look like for you to worship the Father in spirit and truth?

6. **Read John 4:27–42.** How does the woman demonstrate her gratitude and excitement toward believing in Jesus? (Hint: vv. 28–30, 39)

What does a woman serving as the first and very powerful evangelist to the Samaritans communicate about how Jesus views women?

Before the close of John 4, Jesus demonstrates His love and power to yet another kind of person. After meeting a religious Pharisee in the night and a shamed Samaritan woman in broad daylight at the well, He now encounters a heartbroken Gentile father on the border of deep grief.

7. **Read John 4:43–54.** What do you think it was like for a royal official who often gave marching orders to receive marching orders from Jesus? (Hint: v. 50)

Why was the royal official quick to obey?

Why is this second sign or miracle of Jesus significant?

THE
*WORD
BELIEVE
APPEARS
AROUND
* ONE
HUNDRED
TIMES *
* IN
JOHN.

How does this miracle foreshadow Jesus' statement, "I am the resurrection and the life" (John 11:25)?

DAY 3
John 5–6

Jesus journeys back to Jerusalem for a feast. Along the way, He passes by the pool at Bethesda, where He has compassion on a man who has been sick for thirty-eight years.

1. **Read John 5:1–17.** What does Jesus ask the man in verse 6?

   Since most people desire their health, what do you think Jesus was *really* wanting to know from the man?

2. What's the biggest area you've struggled with in your physical, mental, or emotional health?

THIRTY-EIGHT ❋ YEARS WAS LONGER THAN MANY ❋ PEOPLE LIVED IN ❋ ANTIQUITY.

If Jesus asked you the same question in verse 6, how would you respond?

3. **Read John 5:18–47.** What are the main claims Jesus makes within this passage? Why do you think these would anger the religious leaders?

SCRIPTURE	JESUS' CLAIM
John 5:18	*Example: God as His father; making Himself equal with God.*
John 5:24	
John 5:27, 30	
John 5:34	
John 5:36	
John 5:37	
John 5:46–47	

JESUS DOESN'T LOOK TO THE RELIGIOUS LEADERS FOR AFFIRMATION. RATHER HE LOOKS FOR PRAISE THAT COMES FROM THE FATHER.

(V. 44)

4. **Read John 5:39–40.** What is the difference between reading *about* God and actually *knowing* God?

5. When have you been tempted to place more emphasis on reading about God than really knowing God?

   How did you recenter your focus?

6. Reflecting on this week's personal studies, what challenged you the most to really believe in, trust, passionately follow, imitate, and pursue a relationship with Jesus?

7. **Read John 6** to prepare for the next session. Summarize what happens in this chapter in two to three sentences.

How have you experienced Jesus as the Bread of Life?

What are you hungry for in life?

In what areas are you most satisfied with God right now?

reflection

As you reflect on your personal study of John 1–6, what are the BEAUTIFUL WORDS the Holy Spirit has been highlighting to you through this time? Write or draw them in the space below.

SESSION 2

I AM
THE BREAD OF LIFE

John

opening group activity [10-15 MINUTES]

WHAT YOU'LL NEED:

A few different types of bread—including gluten-free and keto-friendly depending on your group's dietary needs

Fun toppings—ranging from butter to veggie spread depending on your group's dietary needs

1. Take a few moments to invite people to sample the breads that agree with their dietary limitations.

2. Discuss the following questions:

   What memory does the smell of freshly-baked bread evoke for you?

   What does it mean to you that Jesus identifies Himself as the Bread of Life?

   What's one question or topic from the homework or discussion that really challenged you or stuck with you?

watch session two video [32 MINUTES]

Leader, play the streaming video or DVD.

As you watch, take notes while thinking through:

What caught your attention?
What surprised you?
What made you reflect?

 Jesus sees the great crowd and has compassion.

✳ We must come hungry.

✳ Jesus partners with a young boy to perform the miracle.

✳ Jesus' response to the chaos is to walk all over it.

✳ The Son of God is the Provider and the Provision.

✳ Every chance Jesus gets, He points all eyes to the Father.

group discussion questions [30–45 MINUTES]

Leader, read each numbered prompt and question to the group and select volunteers for Scripture reading.

"**J**esus invites us to know Him personally, to believe in Him personally: to believe whom He is and what He has done for us, so that we might have life in His name. But first, we must see what we bring . . . and that's a neediness of Him and an awareness of our dependence upon Him. In other words, we must come hungry, aware of our inability to eternally provide what we need for ourselves, let alone for others. Then we must allow that awareness to lead us to depend completely on Him."
—Megan

1. What are some cultural messages that try to convince us that everything depends on us? (Consider recent advertising campaigns or cliches, like "pull yourself up by your bootstraps.") How do these messages contrast with the message of Jesus? On a scale of one to ten, how dependent are you on Christ right now? What is making you more dependent? What is convincing you that you don't need Christ?

2. **Read John 6:5–8 aloud or select a volunteer.** What do Philip's and Andrew's responses have in common? How do they differ? When you approach God with your needs, do you tend to focus more on the problem or the One who can provide? How can being physically, spiritually, or emotionally hungry lead you closer to Jesus? How can it lead others to Jesus?

3. **Read John 6:10–13 aloud to the group.** The small bread and fish don't look like much, but what does Jesus do with them? Describe a time when you brought your small offering—a personal testimony, a meal to a neighbor, an extra car seat, or something you freely gave away—and Jesus did more with it than you expected. What have you been hesitant to share (in time, talents, giftings) because you feel like it's too insignificant or small? How does this encounter with Jesus challenge your thinking? Where is Christ challenging you to simply bring the little you have so God can take your offering and multiply it?

"Jesus reveals that He, Himself, is the living God, the Bread of Life, both the Provider and the Provision. In Jesus, no one will hunger or thirst because He offers eternal life. But this invitation is so much more than a one-time decision. Like the Israelites gathering daily provision from God in the wilderness, the invitation for us is to become dependent on Him and find daily provision for our life through Jesus." Why did God give the Israelites "daily bread"? Why did God create us for hunger in the first place? Do you tend to think of salvation as a one-and-done or an ongoing invitation to daily dependence? Explain. Why is daily dependence on Jesus as the Bread of Life challenging? What are the rewards? —Megan

4. **Select volunteers to read John 6:25–27, 47–51 aloud.** Which food do you spend more energy on: food that spoils or food that endures to eternal life (v. 27)? Which is more rewarding according to Jesus? Why? How can you practice daily dependence on Jesus in the way you spend your time, energy, and focus?

5. Other than Jesus, what do you turn to for satisfaction? What does it look like for you to come to Jesus, receive His provision, believe, and experience the fullness of life?

Jesus is the Bread of Life and all who feast on Him will find the fullness of satisfaction.

close in prayer

Consider the following prompts as you pray together for:

- Willingness to give everything to Jesus
- Trust that Jesus will multiply all we give
- Daily provision and satisfaction in the Bread of Life

preparation

To prepare for the next group session:

1. **Read John 6–8.**
2. Tackle the three days of Session Two Personal Study.
3. Memorize this week's passage using the Beautiful Word Scripture memory coloring page. As a bonus, look up the Scripture memory passage in different translations and take note of the variations.
4. If you've agreed to bring something for the next session's Opening Group Activity, get it ready.

"I am the bread of life. Whoever comes to me will never go hungry, and whoever believes in me will never be thirsty."
—**John 6:35**

PERSONAL STUDY TIME

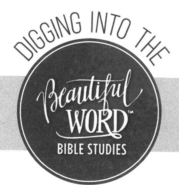

DIGGING INTO THE

Beautiful
WORD™
BIBLE STUDIES

John

I AM THE BREAD OF LIFE

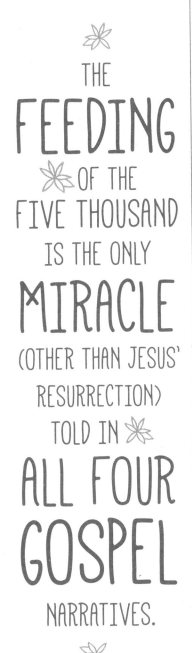

THE FEEDING OF THE FIVE THOUSAND IS THE ONLY MIRACLE (OTHER THAN JESUS' RESURRECTION) TOLD IN ALL FOUR GOSPEL NARRATIVES.

DAY 1
John 6:1-29

John 6 opens with the story of the feeding of the five thousand. Mark and Luke refer to it as a miracle, but, of course, John calls it a sign. Signs always point to something greater, a destination, but the signs are not the destination themselves. The multiplication of food is about more than filling bellies; it's filling hearts and souls with what truly satisfies—knowing and believing Christ through rich, vibrant relationship.

1. **Read John 6:1–14.** Jesus wants us to discover truth for ourselves and not merely rely on what we've heard from others. How does Jesus leverage the situation with the hungry crowds to reveal His compassion to Philip, Andrew, the disciples, the boy, and the crowds?

   What does it reveal about Christ's desire for meaningful relationships that He wants His followers to discover the truth about whom He is for themselves?

2. **Read Psalm 34:8.** What are three specific ways in which you have tasted and seen that the Lord is good?

3. **Read John 6:15 and Luke 5:15–16.** Why does Jesus frequently withdraw to spend time with the Father?

How often do you withdraw to spend time with your Heavenly Father?

What steps can you take to incorporate this practice into your daily life?

4. **Read John 6:16–21.** How does Jesus respond to the chaos of the storm and choppy waters?

What storm or choppy waters do you most need Jesus to walk all over and meet you in the middle of?

IN THE GREEK, JOHN 6:20 CAN BE TRANSLATED,

"AND HE SAYS TO THEM, I AM, DON'T FEAR."

IN ALL KINDS OF SITUATIONS, JESUS REVEALS HIMSELF AS I AM.

5. **Read John 6:22–29.** Why do the crowds pursue Jesus (vv. 26–29)?

6. What does Jesus want to give the people more than physical bread?

   Does anything stop you from believing Jesus wants to give you this, too? If so, describe.

7. Place a check mark (✓) by the top three reasons you pursue Jesus more intently.

   ____ I am in physical need.   ____ I am in emotional need.

   ____ I am in relational need.   ____ I can't do things on my own.

   ____ I long for relationship.   ____ I want to believe.

   ____ I want satisfaction in Him.   ____ I know He is my greatest joy.

   ____ I know the things of this world will never satisfy.

   What does it look like for you to rely on Christ as your daily bread and provider in these areas?

DAY 2
John 6:30-70

The Son of God wants to give the people so much more than food and stuff—Jesus wants to give them Himself, if they will only believe. Like the Israelites, the crowds want provision more than knowing God as provider. They're ready to settle for crumbs when Jesus wants them to experience Him as the Bread of Life.

MANY BELIEVED THAT WHEN THE MESSIAH CAME, THE GIFT OF MANNA WOULD REAPPEAR. THAT'S WHY THE PEOPLE PRESS JESUS TO PROVE HIMSELF BY MAKING MANNA.

1. **Read Exodus 16:1–32 and John 6:30–66.** Fill out the chart below.

SCRIPTURE	QUESTION	RESPONSE
Exodus 16:1–3	What causes the Israelites to grumble?	
John 6:41–43	What causes the crowds surrounding Jesus to grumble?	
Exodus 16:6–12	How does God respond to the Israelites' grumbling?	
John 6:43–51	How does Jesus respond to the crowd's grumbling?	

SCRIPTURE	QUESTION	RESPONSE
Exodus 16:14–19, 23–26	What instructions are given regarding the manna?	
John 6:48–51	What instructions does Jesus give regarding the bread?	
Exodus 16:20, 27	How do some of the Israelites disregard instructions regarding the manna?	
John 6:52, 66	How do some of the crowd disregard Jesus' instruction regarding the bread?	

2. Reflecting on the chart above, why do you think the Israelites struggled to trust God with daily provision?

Reflecting on the chart above, why do you think the crowds struggled to trust Jesus as the Bread of Life and their daily provision?

If you were an Israelite, depending on manna, would you be more tempted to stockpile manna or try to gather when you were told there wouldn't be any? Why?

How are you tempted to stockpile resources or over-gather now?

How can you practice outrageous generosity instead?

3. Reflecting on the chart, why do you think the crowds struggled to trust and believe Jesus was who He said He was?

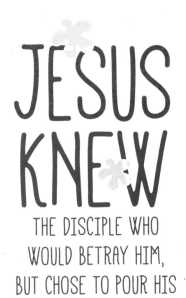

JESUS KNEW THE DISCIPLE WHO WOULD BETRAY HIM, BUT CHOSE TO POUR HIS LOVE, TIME, AND PRESENCE INTO THE DISCIPLE ANYWAY, REVEALING THE VULNERABLE, COMPASSIONATE HEART OF GOD (VV. 70–71).

4. What's the biggest way you've been struggling to trust Jesus as the Bread of Life, your daily provision, and the satisfaction your soul craves?

5. **Read John 6:66.** What does this tell us about those who turned away (1 John 2:19)?

What are the characteristics of those who are true followers of Jesus (John 14:23)?

6. **Read John 6:67–70.** How does Simon Peter's response to Jesus' teaching differ from the crowds?

How would you answer Jesus' question in verse 67?

7. Trace back to the chapter's opening story of feeding the multitudes, and the role of neediness to discovering God. In the space below, write two to three sentences about what it truly means for you to need, believe, and experience Christ as the Bread of Life.

DAY 3
John 7–8

Between chapters 6 and 7, a dramatic shift takes place. Jesus teaches that without eating His flesh and drinking His blood, there's no real life (6:53–54). With those words, a spiritual threshold is crossed in which the religious leaders and crowds respond with increasing animosity. Jesus is not deterred.

1. **Read John 7:1–13.** What do Jesus' brothers pressure Him to do?

How does Jesus respond?

How does Jesus' response demonstrate John 5:19?

What spiritual practices help you stay in tune with what God is calling you to do? (Examples: reading God's Word, sabbath, prayer, fasting, confession, fellowship)

2. **Read John 7:1–24.** How does Jesus redirect glory to His Father?

What can you learn from Jesus about redirecting glory to God?

What difference would this make in your life with respect to your perspective on your own worth and importance?

Some people listening to Jesus begin believing and placing their faith in Him. This only angers the religious leaders more.

3. **Read John 7:25–36.** How do the people respond to Jesus?

What surprises you about their response?

4. **Read John 7:37–44.** Where do you most need to experience the living waters of Christ right now?

5. **Read John 7:45–52.** How does Nicodemus respond to his colleagues, the religious leaders?

6. What does this suggest about the lasting impact of Nicodemus' encounter with Jesus in chapter 3?

"COME, ALL YOU WHO ARE **THIRSTY**, COME TO THE **WATERS**;

AND YOU WHO HAVE **NO MONEY**, COME, BUY AND EAT!"

—**Isaiah 55:1**

7. **Read John 8** to prepare for the next session. Summarize what happens in this chapter in two to three sentences.

How have you experienced Jesus as the Light of the World?

What's one area of your life where you long for the light of Christ to break in?

Ask Him to break in now. He will. He wants to.

reflection

As you reflect on your personal study of John 6–8, what are BEAUTIFUL WORDS the Holy Spirit has been highlighting to you through this time? Write or draw them in the space below.

I AM
THE LIGHT OF
THE WORLD

John

opening group activity

WHAT YOU'LL NEED:

A few different types of light sources. Be creative. Suggestions include a flashlight, a small lamp, a string of lights, and a few candles.

1. Turn on each light source in a place participants can view them.

2. Take a few moments to dim overall light in the room and invite participants to write down a few observations about what they see, think, and feel when they look at the lights.

3. Discuss the following questions:

   Which of the light sources are most comforting to you? Which of the light sources are least comforting? What made the difference?

   What comes to mind when you think of Jesus as the Light of the World?

   What draws you to Jesus as the Light of the World?

watch session three video [24 MINUTES]

Leader, play the streaming video or DVD.

As you watch, take notes while thinking through:

What caught your attention?
What surprised you?
What made you reflect?

✳ The Feast of Tabernacles always had a lot of lights.

The light represents the presence of God.

 The Light of the World leads, guides, and exposes.

Jesus doesn't expose the woman, but rather the men holding the rocks.

The problem isn't out there, it's inside us.

We're mirrors reflecting God's glory.

SCRIPTURE covered in this session:
John 8

group discussion questions [30-45 MINUTES]

Leader, read each numbered prompt and question to the group and select volunteers for
Scripture reading.

1. **Read John 8:1–11 aloud to the group.** What surprises you most about Jesus' response to
   the woman? As the Light of the World, who does Jesus expose in this encounter? What
   does this reveal about God's heart toward your areas of shame? Areas of judgmentalism?
   Who is someone you've been treating like the woman who committed adultery? How can
   you change your attitude and response to reflect Christ?

   "The whole purpose of the feast was to remind present and future generations of the ways God provided supernaturally in the desert during the exodus. In John 6, Jesus proclaims, 'I am the bread of life' (6:35). Then in John 7, Jesus declares, 'Let anyone who is thirsty come to me and drink' (7:37). And here, in this context, Jesus identifies Himself as not only the miraculous bread and the water of heaven, but the light representing the presence of God (John 8:12)." —Megan

2. What does it mean to you that Jesus is the Light of the World? How has believing in Jesus
   helped you walk in the light instead of the darkness?

3. Select volunteers to **read Genesis 1:3, John 1:1–5, and John 8:12 aloud.** What do these
   passages have in common? How does Jesus' declaration in 8:12 reveal whom He is and
   whom He has always been? Where do you need Christ's light?

"**J**esus, the Light, invites us to a different path than the world, to open up our lives, let darkness be exposed to the light of Christ . . . to open up our heart and discover how Christ may be wanting to transform us more into His likeness. It's like Jesus is saying to the Pharisees, 'the problem isn't out there, it's in here.'" —Megan

What do you agree with in Megan's teaching? With what do you disagree? Do you tend to look for problems "out there" or "in here" more? Which is harder to look at? Why?

4. What's one area where you sense the Spirit leading you to take a hard look at your attitudes, actions, and responses? What hope do you have in allowing Christ's light to shine in your darkness?

5. **Read Ephesians 5:8–14.** If appropriate, take a few moments to dim the light in the room and turn on a single small light. Use this time of silence to ask the Holy Spirit to reveal where the Spirit is calling you to be a child of the light, whose fruit consists of goodness, righteousness, and truth. Then share what you thought about.

Jesus is the Light of the World and all who follow Him will not walk in darkness.

close in prayer

Consider the following prompts as you pray together for:

- Hearts sensitive to the work of the Spirit

- Opportunities to experience the light of Christ

- Opportunities to shine the light of Christ

preparation

To prepare for the next group session:

1. **Read John 8–10.**

2. Tackle the three days of Session Three Personal Study.

3. Memorize this week's passage using the Beautiful Word Scripture memory coloring page. As a bonus, look up the Scripture memory passage in different translations and take note of the variations.

4. If you agreed to bring something for the next session's Opening Group Activity, make sure to have it ready.

"I am the light of the world. Whoever follows me will never walk in darkness, but will have the light of life."

—John 8:12

PERSONAL STUDY TIME

DIGGING INTO THE

Beautiful WORD™

BIBLE STUDIES

John

I AM THE LIGHT OF THE WORLD

DAY 1
John 8:1–30

The scribes and Pharisees, who believe following all the rules will save them, bring a woman to Jesus and ask a tough question.

1. **Read John 8:1–11.** Were the religious leaders trying to get at Jesus, the woman, or both?

   What does this reveal about how religion rules can make you hardhearted and judgmental?

2. Reflecting on how Jesus responded to the woman, how can you better respond to that person?

3. **Read John 8:12–30.** Describe a time in the past when you walked in darkness.

JESUS' CALL TO "LEAVE YOUR LIFE OF SIN" (V. 11) IS SOMETIMES TRANSLATED, "SIN NO MORE."

4. How were you able to break through and begin walking in the light?

5. Long before Jesus identified Himself as the Light of the World, God revealed Himself as light. God illuminates our paths and calls His children to share His light. Look up the following passages and fill in the chart below.

SCRIPTURE	HOW GOD IS REVEALED AS LIGHT
Exodus 13:22	
Psalm 27:1	
Psalm 119:105	

The Pharisees **try to discredit Jesus' claim** to be the Light of the World based on lack of witnesses **(Numbers 35:30 and Deuteronomy 17:6).**

Jesus counters that He is uniquely qualified to testify to this truth because of **His relationship with the Father.**

SCRIPTURE	HOW GOD IS REVEALED AS LIGHT
Isaiah 42:6–7	
Malachi 4:2	

6. How have you experienced Jesus personally as the guiding light of God sent from heaven?

7. **Read Matthew 5:16.** How do you sense the Spirit challenging you to live this out in your daily life?

DAY 2
John 8:31–59

The debate between the religious leaders and Jesus intensifies as they refuse to accept the deep truths Jesus reveals about Himself. Toward the end, they even suggest Jesus is demon-possessed. Meanwhile, Jesus says that rather than acting like Abraham's descendants, they're behaving more like the devil's children.

1. **Read John 8:31–32.** What claim does Jesus make?

   How do you think truth sets us free?

2. On the continuum below, how free are you in Christ? Who is more concerned about your freedom—God or you?

   ①←②–③–④–⑤–⑥–⑦–⑧–⑨→⑩

   I have a lot   I've experienced
   of areas   the freedom
   I don't feel   of Christ in every
   free in Christ.   area of my life.

   What's one area in which you long to experience the freedom of Christ?

Write a prayer in the space below asking Christ to set you free.

3. **Read John 8:33–59.** The religious leaders claim God and Abraham as their father. How do their attitudes and actions contradict their claims according to Jesus? (Hint: vv. 39–47)

4. It's easy to think of someone whose claims about knowing God were contradicted by their attitudes and actions and much harder to notice this tendency in ourselves. Describe a time when your claims about knowing God were contradicted by your attitudes and actions.

5. Take a moment to prayerfully ask the Holy Spirit to reveal any areas of your life that don't align with your desire to know God or believe in Jesus. Write anything that comes to mind in the space below.

FREEDOM IN CHRIST IS NOT A PERMISSION SLIP TO DO ANYTHING YOU DESIRE, BUT RATHER THE JOYOUS PRIVILEGE OF DOING WHAT'S RIGHT IN ALIGNMENT WITH GOD.

6. What does Jesus' proclamation in John 8:58, "Before Abraham was born, I am!" tell us about Him (also see Exodus 3:14)?

7. Why did this proclamation in verse 58 lead to their response in verse 59?

DAY 3
John 9–10

In chapter 8, Jesus leverages an encounter with a woman who committed adultery to challenge and correct some of the false beliefs of the religious leaders. Now, Jesus exposes some of the disciples' false beliefs through the healing of a man born blind.

1. **Read John 9:1–12.** What do the disciples (and religious leaders) misunderstand about the man's inability to see? What mistaken presuppositions were driving their conclusion?

"I BELIEVE IN CHRISTIANITY AS I BELIEVE THAT THE SUN HAS RISEN: NOT ONLY BECAUSE I SEE IT, BUT BECAUSE BY IT I SEE EVERYTHING ELSE."

—C.S. LEWIS

THE POOL OF SILOAM (V. 7) CAN BE TRANSLATED THE POOL OF THE SENT. THE ROLE OF THE AQUEDUCT THAT CARRIED THE WATER BECAME THE NAME OF THE POOL. JUST AS THE WATER WAS SENT TO CREATE THE POOL,

CHRIST WAS SENT TO BRING SATISFACTION TO THOSE THIRSTING FOR GOD.

2. When you see someone suffering, what or whom are you most tempted to blame? (Ex. the person's or families' poor choices, a fallen world, lack of faith?)

How does what you blame affect your readiness to get involved, bring healing, and pray?

3. Which *I Am* statement does Jesus repeat from John 8:12? (Hint: v. 5)

Jesus opens the eyes of the man born blind and literally brings light into his life. This contrasts sharply with the response of the Pharisees and exposes who is living in the darkness and spiritually blind.

4. **Read John 9:13–34.** Fill in the chart below. How do those who witness and experience the miracle respond?

WITNESSES	SCRIPTURE	RESPONSE
The Pharisees	John 9:13–17, 28–34	
The Parents	John 9:18–23	
The Man	John 9:24–34	

5. How would you respond if you experienced or witnessed this miracle?

6. **Read John 9:35–41.** What does Jesus reveal about belief in Him during His second encounter with the man?

7. **Read John 10** to prepare for the next session. Summarize what happens in this chapter in two to three sentences.

How have you experienced Jesus as the Good Shepherd?

What might it look like to make an upcoming decision with the Lord as your shepherd? Be specific with a decision you're being faced with in your answer.

Is there an area of your life where you doubt or question that Jesus is the Good Shepherd?

reflection

As you reflect on your personal study of John 8–10, what are the BEAUTIFUL WORDS the Holy Spirit has been highlighting to you through this time? Write or draw them in the space below.

I AM

THE GATE AND
THE GOOD SHEPHERD

John

opening group activity [10–15 MINUTES]

WHAT YOU'LL NEED:

A few different types of sheep images or décor such as sheep artwork, toy sheep, carved sheep, etc.

1. Display the sheep images and art where participants can view and interact with the items.

2. Discuss the following questions:

   Which is your favorite sheep? Why?

   Read Psalm 23 aloud. Where do you most need to experience and trust Jesus as your Good Shepherd now?

   What's one question or topic from the homework or discussion that really challenged you or stuck with you?

watch session four video [25 MINUTES]

Leader, play the streaming video or DVD.

As you watch, take notes while thinking through:

What caught your attention?
What surprised you?
What made you reflect?

❋ When it comes to remembering names, I just wasn't prioritizing it.

✳ There is a difference between true shepherds and bad ones.

✳ You can tell the true King the same way you can tell the true Shepherd.

✳ The thief seeks to steal our hearts and affection.

✳ There are only two types of people in the word: those who need Jesus, and, well, Jesus.

✳ The shepherd doesn't lead the sheep anywhere He isn't willing to go first.

SCRIPTURE covered in this session:
John 10

group discussion questions [30-45 MINUTES]

Leader, read each numbered prompt and question to the group and select volunteers for Scripture reading.

1. **Read John 10:1–5 aloud.** What characteristics describe the true Shepherd? Which characteristics describe the sheep?

2. In verse 4, where are the sheep in relationship to the Shepherd and why is this significant? What is the key factor of trust we see in verses 4 and 5? What does "know His voice" presuppose—that He is speaking? How can you purposefully listen for the voice of God in your prayer times?

3. Why do the sheep follow the Shepherd? Describe a time when you sensed you were being led by God. What was the result? As you consider how He has led you, how would you describe His tone (calm, urgent, kind, demanding)? What helps you be more sensitive to the Shepherd's voice? Where do you sense the Shepherd's voice leading you now?

"The sheep pen was an enclosure with walls and no roof that would often have the sheep of an entire village kept within. After the sheep were brought in for the night, it was common for the shepherd to sleep at the entrance so he could protect his sheep. To be with them. To be near them. To comfort. To give them life." What do you think it means for Jesus to identify Himself as "the gate for the sheep" (v. 7)? —Megan

4. **Read John 10:7–15 aloud.** What is the mission of the thief and the hired hand? What is the mission of the Good Shepherd? Describe a time when you sensed the thief was wreaking havoc on your life. How did or didn't you allow the Good Shepherd to help restore you?

5. **Read Psalm 23 as a group aloud as prayer.** What are the verbs or action words mentioned in this passage? Which of these do you most need to experience now?

"The shepherd doesn't lead the sheep anywhere He isn't first willing to go." How does this promise give you comfort in the challenges you're facing?
—Megan

Jesus is the Gate and the Good Shepherd leading you to the abundant life.

close in prayer

Consider the following prompts as you pray together to:

- Intimately know Jesus as the Gate and the Good Shepherd

- Grow in trusting the Good Shepherd to let Him lead

- Experience God's voice in a personal, specific, and meaningful way

1. **Read John 10–11.**

2. Tackle the three days of Session Four Personal Study.

3. Memorize this week's passage using the Beautiful Word Scripture memory coloring page. As a bonus, look up the Scripture memory passage in different translations and take note of the variations.

4. If you've agreed to bring something for the next session's Opening Group Activity, get it ready.

"Very truly I tell you, I am the gate for the sheep . . . I am the good shepherd. The good shepherd lays down his life for the sheep."
—John 10:7, 11

PERSONAL
STUDY TIME

DIGGING INTO THE

Beautiful
WORD™
BIBLE STUDIES

John
I AM THE GATE AND THE GOOD SHEPHERD

DAY 1
John 10:1–10

Jesus draws on rich imagery of sheep and shepherding found throughout the Old Testament to reveal God's heart. In an agrarian world, the realities of caring for sheep would have been well-known to the disciples and all who heard His teaching.

1. **Read John 10:1–6.** Who does Jesus address in this opening verse?

What is Jesus warning the religious leaders?

How do the religious leaders respond? (Hint: v. 6)

Sheep were kept in an enclosed space, likely made of stone, near the shepherd's home for their protection. The pens had an opening that could be closed by a gate made of briars or branches. Those who climbed over the wall rather than going through the gate used deception and likely came to take the sheep by force.

2. **Reflecting on John 10:2–6,** fill in the chart below. How does the one who climbs over the gate compare to the one who enters by the gate?

CHARACTERISTICS OF THE ONE WHO CLIMBS OVER THE GATE	CHARACTERISTICS OF THE ONE WHO COMES THROUGH THE GATE

3. In two to three sentences, how would you summarize the attitudes and actions of a genuine shepherd?

4. What helps you recognize the Spirit's voice and leading in your life?

WHEN JESUS SAYS ALL WHO CAME BEFORE HIM ARE **THIEVES AND ROBBERS**, HE IS NOT SPEAKING OF MOSES, ABRAHAM, OR THE ANCIENT HEROES OF FAITH WHOM HE COMMENDS. RATHER, JESUS IS DESCRIBING THOSE WHO ARE PART OF THE **RELIGIOUS ESTABLISHMENT** AND USE PIETY FOR PERSONAL GAIN.

5. Describe a time when you heard or encountered the voice of God in your life as He led you by His Spirit. What was the result?

6. **Read John 10:6–10.** What promises does Jesus give to those who enter through the gate?

   What do you think Jesus means by "be saved" in this context?

7. How have you experienced protection, provision, and nourishment through your relationship with Jesus?

DAY 2
John 10:11–21

After identifying Himself as the Gate, Jesus now reveals Himself using one of the richest, most beautiful, and endearing images in all the Bible: the Good Shepherd.

1. **Read John 10:11–13.** Fill in the chart below. How does the Shepherd differ from the hireling?

CHARACTERISTICS OF THE GOOD SHEPHERD	CHARACTERISTICS OF THE HIRELING

2. What do the characteristics of the Good Shepherd reveal about the relationship Jesus desires with you?

THE GREEK WORD **GINOSKO** (MEANING "TO KNOW") APPEARS FOUR TIMES IN JOHN 10:14–15. THIS KIND OF KNOWLEDGE IS NOT **PROPOSITIONAL** BUT **RELATIONAL** KNOWLEDGE. IT'S NOT KNOWING ABOUT SOMETHING BUT AN INTIMATE CONNECTION WITH AND UNDERSTANDING OF SOMEONE. THE BOND OF RELATIONSHIP BETWEEN **SHEPHERD** AND **SHEEP** IS PARALLEL TO **FATHER** AND **SON**—THEY TRULY KNOW EACH OTHER INTIMATELY.

3. What holds you back from believing Jesus and going deeper in your relationship with Him? Write your response as a prayer in the space below.

4. **Read Psalm 23.** What specific actions does the Shepherd take with the sheep?

How have you experienced Jesus, the Good Shepherd, responding in the same ways with you?

5. **Read John 10:14.** After Jesus repeats that He is the Good Shepherd, what does Jesus say?

What comfort do you find in knowing that Jesus knows you better than anyone else?

How do you know that you know Jesus?

6. **Read John 10:15–18.** How does Jesus demonstrate His love for His sheep?

What is one way God is leading you to practice sacrificial love?

What's holding you back? Who in your life spurs you on to love sacrificially?

7. **Read John 10:19–21.** How do those listening to Jesus respond?

What surprises you most about their responses?

What do their responses reveal about their hearts toward Jesus and experiencing Him as the Good Shepherd?

DAY 3
John 10:22–42

The Feast of Dedication or Hanukkah celebrates the recapturing of the temple. It's also known as the Feast of Lights, because when the priests reentered the temple, they found the holy oil miraculously provided enough fuel for eight days. In this passage, Jewish adversaries approach Jesus to question Him.

1. **Read John 10:22–42.** What promises does Jesus give to His sheep?

How does this passage echo what Jesus has already said about Himself?

2. In the space below, write down every phrase that speaks to belief or believing from this passage.

Why is Jesus so concerned with belief and believing in Him?

How has believing in Christ changed your life?

How has your understanding of believing in Jesus changed since you began studying John?

3. **Read John 11** to prepare for the next session. Summarize what happens in this chapter in two to three sentences.

What fills you with the most hope from this chapter?

How have you experienced Jesus bringing you to a fuller life?

MY FATHER, WHO HAS GIVEN THEM TO ME, IS GREATER THAN ALL; NO ONE CAN SNATCH THEM OUT OF MY FATHER'S HAND.

— JOHN 10:29

reflection

As you reflect on your personal study of John 10–11, what are the BEAUTIFUL WORDS the Holy Spirit has been highlighting to you through this time? Write or draw them in the space below.

I AM
THE RESURRECTION AND THE LIFE

John

opening group activity [10–15 MINUTES]

WHAT YOU'LL NEED:

A music player (such as a smart phone) with a downloaded playlist so you are ready to play a song that speaks of Jesus as the Resurrection and the Life such as "Resurrection Power" or "Forever."

1. Listen or sing along to the selected song. Consider printing out or providing a link to the lyrics.

2. Discuss the following questions:

   How have you experienced the resurrection power of Christ?

   How has your life changed or expanded because of Jesus?

   What's one way you've experienced the abundant life Jesus promises?

watch session five video [30 MINUTES]

Leader, play the streaming video or DVD.

As you watch, take notes while thinking through:

What caught your attention?
What surprised you?
What made you reflect?

❋ Jesus knew all along that Lazarus was not going to stay dead.

* Jesus knows what He's doing and why.

* Jesus wants to give them resurrection life.

* Jesus has a better plan.

* Out walks Lazarus, four days dead.

* Many believed, but many more were mad.

SCRIPTURE covered in this session:
John 11

group discussion questions [30–45 MINUTES]

Leader, read each numbered prompt and question to the group and select volunteers for Scripture reading.

1. **Select a volunteer to read John 11:1–6 aloud to the group.** What surprises you most about Jesus' response to the news of Lazarus's sickness? Why doesn't Jesus rush to Lazarus's side? Share a time of pain, loss, or disappointment when nothing seemed to make sense, but afterward, you discovered God's faithfulness. How can this experience impact your trust in Jesus?

> "Jesus knew all and He knows all. He knows every hair on your head and the words on your tongue even before you speak them. He is outside of time. He's already at the place of the person you're becoming. There's nowhere you can go where the Spirit of God cannot reach you or find you." —Megan

2. What comfort does this bring you? When are you most tempted to forget or doubt these truths?

3. **Select volunteers to read John 11:7–13 aloud to the group.** How does Jesus show that seeing God for whom He truly is and worshiping Him is more important than the life of Lazarus? On a scale of one to ten, how hard is it for you to accept that belief in Jesus is everything?

4. **Select volunteers to read John 11:20–27 aloud to the group.** How would you describe Martha's response to Jesus? What does Martha misunderstand about the resurrection? Do you tend to think of the resurrection as a past event, future event, or the person of Jesus Christ? Why?

How does Jesus' *I Am* statement (v. 25) change the way you view life and death? How does this statement help us understand Jesus better?

5. **Select volunteers to read John 11:32–46.** What do you think about verse 35? What does Jesus' response toward Lazarus reveal about God's tenderheartedness toward you? In what ways are you, too, sitting in the days between Lazarus' death and resurrection? Where do you most acutely feel the tension that all things have not been made right yet? How do you live in that tension?

"Whom Jesus revealed Himself to be, through this *I Am* statement, is more significant than what He did. Jesus resurrected Lazarus as a sign to reveal to Mary, Martha, everyone around, and everyone who has read this passage since, Jesus is more than a healer, He conquers death through Resurrection life." —Megan

6. How does "I am the Resurrection and the Life" expand what you know about Jesus? How does "I am the Resurrection and the Life" change what you believe about Jesus? How does it bring you hope for the future and comfort in the present? In what ways does Jesus' raising of Lazarus from the dead foreshadow His own death and resurrection?

Jesus is more than a healer; He conquers death through Resurrection life.

close in prayer

Consider the following prompts as you pray together for:

- Deeper, more vibrant belief in Jesus
- The fullness of the power of the resurrection in our lives
- Opportunities to live for the glory of God

preparation

To prepare for the next group session:

1. **Read John 11–14.**

2. Tackle the three days of Session Five Personal Study.

3. Memorize this week's passage using the Beautiful Word Scripture memory coloring page. As a bonus, look up the Scripture memory passage in different translations and take note of the variations.

4. If you've agreed to bring something for the next session's Opening Group Activity, get it ready.

"'I am the resurrection and the
life. The one who believes in me
will live, even though they die.'"
—John 11:25

PERSONAL STUDY TIME

DIGGING INTO THE
Beautiful
WORD™
BIBLE STUDIES

John

I AM THE RESURRECTION AND THE LIFE

DAY 1
John 11

The death and raising of Lazarus mark a significant turn in the Gospel of John. This miracle sets in motion a series of events that lead to the arrest and crucifixion of Jesus (11:53).

1. **Read John 11:1–15.** What details from this passage suggest Jesus was close to Lazarus, Martha, and Mary?

What does Jesus' refusal to rush toward Lazarus reveal about His claim that He only does what He sees the Father doing (John 5:19)? What does it say about the sovereignty of God—and the trust He wants us to have in His sovereignty?

THE NAME
LAZARUS
MEANS
"WHOM
GOD
HELPS."

2. **Read John 11:16–27.** What does this passage reveal about Jesus' identity and mission?

How have you experienced Jesus as the Resurrection and the Life?

3. **Read John 11:27–44.** What role does belief have in this passage? (Hint: vv. 40, 42)

How does Lazarus emerge from the tomb? (Hint: v. 44)

Who in your life needs to know that Jesus is the Resurrection and the Life? Write your response as a prayer below.

4. **Read John 11:45–46.** What are the different responses people have to the miracle?

If you had witnessed the miracle, how do you think you would have responded? Why?

How can you presently respond to the powerful and unmistakable work of God in either your own or someone else's life today?

5. **Read John 11:47–57.** How and why does opposition to Jesus increase following this miracle?

6. What are the chief priests and Pharisees most concerned about when it comes to Jesus? (Hint: v. 48)

7. In what areas of your life are you tempted to cling to power and position right now?

What would it look like to be set free from these unhealthy attachments?

DAY 2
John 12

In this chapter, Jesus's public ministry transitions to a more private one with His closest followers. Jesus knows the return to Jerusalem will result in His execution.

1. **Read John 12:1–11.** What significance does Jesus attach to Mary's actions? (Hint: 12:7)

What is most beautiful and most challenging about Mary's actions?

● Most beautiful:

● Most challenging:

How does Jesus' and Judas' response to Mary differ?

What does each response reveal about what they truly believe?

2. **Read John 12:12–19, Zechariah 9:9, and Psalm 118:27.**
   How do the details of Jesus' entrance reveal Him as the long-awaited Messiah?

How do the multitudes respond to Jesus? The Pharisees?

How do the Pharisees double down on their resolve to destroy Jesus?

JESUS SAYS HIS SOUL IS TROUBLED (12:27). IN THE **GREEK**, TROUBLED IS **TARASSO**, MEANING TO CAUSE ACUTE **EMOTIONAL DISTRESS.**

3. **Read John 12:20–26.** What is Jesus calling you to give up, walk away from, or die to so that the life of Christ may be more fully displayed in you?

4. **Read John 12:27–32.** Describe the mission of Jesus in one to two sentences based on this passage.

5. **Read John 12:33–43.** Make a list of all the reasons people refuse to believe in Jesus from this passage. Which of these do you struggle with most?

How does refusing to believe in Jesus affect one's spiritual senses?

Throughout the **Bible,** the **voice of God** is often connected with **thunder**

(John 12:29; Psalm 18:13; Ezekiel 3:12; Job 40:9; and Revelation 14:2).

The Gospel of John now records Jesus' final public message before His arrest.

6. **Read John 12:44–50.** Which verses in this passage echo what Jesus has been teaching throughout the Gospel of John?

7. What stands out to you from Jesus' final words?

DAY 3
John 13–14

With the full knowledge that He will be arrested soon, Jesus spends His final free hours with His followers—loving, serving, and encouraging them—for what is about to take place. In antiquity, foot washing was reserved for the lowliest servants. Peers didn't wash other peers' feet. The disciples could never imagine allowing Jesus, their rabbi, to wash their feet. Yet He does.

1. **Read John 13:1–11.** What spiritual lessons is Jesus teaching the disciples by washing their feet?

What does Jesus' willingness to wash all the disciples' feet, including Judas, reveal about the bounds of His love?

What area of your life do you need Jesus to tenderly hold and cleanse for you?

2. **Read John 13:12–20.** Just as Jesus selflessly served others by washing their feet, He is giving us an example to follow. There are many ways we, too, can selflessly serve others—outside of the obvious one of foot washing. What are some ways you have selflessly served others this week?

Who in your life have you avoided serving? What can you do to serve that person?

3. **Read John 13:21–32.** How are both the Son and the Father glorified through the betrayal?

THROUGH THE
FOOT
WASHING,
JESUS TEACHES
THROUGH BOTH
WORD AND
ACTION.

AS YOU READ THE STORIES OF JESUS, IT'S IMPORTANT TO NOTE BOTH WHAT HE SAYS AND WHAT HE DOES.

4. Think of a time someone has betrayed you.

On the continuum below, mark how close you are to forgiving the person.

❶ ← ❷ – ❸ – ❹ – ❺ – ❻ – ❼ – ❽ – ❾ → ❿

I can't stand
the thought
of forgiving
the person.

I've fully
forgiven and
that person has
no power over me.

Forgiveness sounds wonderful until we're asked to give it away. We want God to forgive us, others to forgive us, and yet we're not quick to forgive others. What's worse, we're not sure we want God to forgive them . . . because they hurt us. It's easy to get caught up believing that having them suffering for what they've done will somehow make us feel better or set us free. It won't. Only forgiveness can do that. Unforgiveness is like drinking poison hoping the other person dies. Take a moment and consider Jesus washing Judas' feet and write out a prayer, thanking Him for the power of forgiveness, asking Him to help you respond to betrayal through the power of His Spirit in you.

5. **Read John 13:33–38.** What is the new commandment Jesus gives? (Hint: v. 34)

What is the result of living the new command? (Hint: v. 35)

How are you working with the Holy Spirit to fulfill this new command?

6. What's one relationship in which you're not fulfilling this new command?

What steps do you sense the Holy Spirit is inviting you to take to change your attitude and actions?

How might remembering Jesus' love for you help you love others?

7. **Read John 14** to prepare for the next session. Summarize what happens in this chapter in two to three sentences.

What fills you with the most hope from this chapter?

How have you experienced Jesus as the Way, the Truth, and the Life?

reflection

As you reflect on your personal study of John 11–14, what are the BEAUTIFUL WORDS the Holy Spirit has been highlighting to you through this time? Write or draw them in the space below.

I AM

THE WAY, THE TRUTH, AND THE LIFE

John

opening group activity [10-15 MINUTES]

WHAT YOU'LL NEED:

Pens or pencils

1. Using the chart provided, mark the first column, "The Way," the second column, "The Truth," and the third column, "The Life."

2. Spend two to three minutes in prayer asking the Holy Spirit how Jesus has revealed Himself to you in each of these ways. Make a list under each column heading in answer to:

    How have you encountered Jesus as "the way"?

    How have you encountered Jesus as "the truth"?

    How have you encountered Jesus as "the life"?

3. Discuss what has been and is being revealed to you that is new or taking you by surprise.

    What's one question or topic from the homework or discussion that really challenged you or stuck with you?

watch session six video [27 MINUTES]

Leader, play the streaming video or DVD.

As you watch, take notes while thinking through:

What caught your attention?
What surprised you?
What made you reflect?

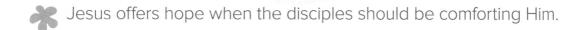 Jesus offers hope when the disciples should be comforting Him.

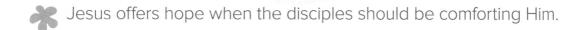 The disciples never imagine the Messiah will come only to soon leave.

✳ One day we will be in the presence of Jesus face to face.

✳ Truth is not our possession, it's His possession.

✳ The only way to experience eternal life is through Jesus, the source of salvation.

✳ It's not the size of our faith that matters but the object of our faith.

SCRIPTURE covered in this session:
John 14

group discussion questions [30-45 MINUTES]

Leader, read each numbered prompt and question to the group and select volunteers for Scripture reading.

1. **Read John 14:1–7.** What do you think the Father's house will be like? Why? What encourages you most from this passage? What do Jesus' preparations reveal about His love for you?

> "When Jesus claims to be 'the way,' He is describing the way to His Father. It is not that He knows the way, it is that He *is* the way. There is no other way to be reconciled to God. Eternal life is found in Jesus only! Notice, Jesus doesn't say I am *a way* or I've laid out *a path*. No, He is *the* way." —Megan

2. What comfort do you find in Jesus identifying Himself as "The Way"? Describe a way in which people struggle with Jesus' claim to be the way.

> "Jesus is saying the source of all truth, the standard by which truth is measured. He is equating Himself with the Law of God, as the Arbiter of truth and righteousness. In Him, there is nothing that is false, or uncertain, or misleading. He embodies truth." —Megan

3. What's easy for you to accept in this statement? What's more challenging? How do you think about and respond to people who say, "This is my truth"?

4. How have you experienced Jesus as "The Life"? What's one area where you'd like to experience more of the life of Jesus?

"It's tempting to hear these words from Jesus about being the Way, the Truth, and the Life, and think they only apply presently to our unbelieving neighbors, friends, family members. No! These truths are not just for unbelievers but believers. We need Jesus to be the Way, the Truth, and the Life daily." —Megan

5. In your daily routines, where do you live as if God accepts you based on *what you do* rather than what *He has done*?

6. On a scale of one to ten, how often are you tempted to believe that God loves you more on the days we perform well for Him (read Scripture, attend church, pray, etc.)? Have you thought, "God forgives me, but I just can't forgive myself"? Whose standard have you diminished in those thoughts? Where do you most need to experience Jesus as the Way, the Truth, and the Life to walk in greater wholeness and freedom?

The gospel is not about what we do or how large our faith is; it's all about Jesus—the Way, the Truth, and the Life.

close in prayer

Consider the following prompts as you pray together for:

- Hope in Jesus for what He's preparing

- Heightened awareness of Jesus as the Way, the Truth, and the Life

- Anticipation for the day we see Jesus face to face

preparation

To prepare for the next group session:

1. **Read John 14–15.**

2. Tackle the three days of Session Six Personal Study Time.

3. Memorize this week's passage using the Beautiful Word Scripture memory coloring page. As a bonus, look up the Scripture memory passage in different translations and take note of the variations.

"'I am
the way
and the
truth and
the life.
No one
comes
to the
Father
except
through
me.'"

—John 14:6

PERSONAL
STUDY TIME

DIGGING INTO THE

Beautiful
WORD™
BIBLE STUDIES

John

I AM THE WAY, THE TRUTH, AND THE LIFE

DAY 1
John 14:1–6

On the night of His arrest, Jesus comforts His disciples and admonishes them. He promises that the Advocate, the Holy Spirit (14:26) is coming.

1. **Read John 14:1.** What does Jesus prescribe for those whose hearts are troubled?

   How is your heart troubled right now?

   How does believing in Christ bring calmness and peace?

2. **Read John 14:2–3.** How does Jesus show His love for His disciples?

3. How do these opening verses of John 14 encourage you?

4. What do the following passages reveal about the promised heavenly home? Which makes you the most excited? Why?

SCRIPTURE	DETAILS OF THE PRESENCE OF GOD AND HEAVEN
Revelation 7:9	
Revelation 21:9–12	
Revelation 22:1–5	

5. What comfort do you find in reflecting on the heavenly home Jesus has prepared for you?

6. **Read John 14:4–6.** Why is it important to believe that Jesus is *the* way instead of *a* way?

7. How do you graciously respond to others who view Jesus as one of many ways to God?

8. Reflecting on the encouragement and comfort Jesus gives His disciples, who is someone you can reach out to encourage and comfort?

JESUS SAID, "IF YOU HOLD TO MY TEACHING, YOU ARE REALLY MY DISCIPLES. THEN YOU WILL KNOW THE TRUTH, AND THE TRUTH WILL SET YOU FREE."

— JOHN 8:31B–32

DAY 2
John 14:7–15

Jesus knows some of the disciples are still struggling with His teaching. He takes time to affirm them in the truth of whom He is. More than anything, Jesus wants His disciples to know and believe fully in Him.

1. **Read John 14:8–10.** After spending three years with Jesus, what does Philip still not realize about Jesus? (Hint: v. 8)

2. If you know Jesus, you know God (14:7–11) because Jesus is God. On the continuum below, how well do you know Jesus?

④ I know and trust Jesus intimately.

↑

③ I know a lot about Jesus.

|

② I know a little about Jesus.

↓

① I don't know Jesus.

3. Do you think it is possible to know Jesus without knowing God? Why or why not?

How do Jesus' words challenge you to see Jesus and the Father as one?

4. **Read John 14:10–11.** Reflecting on this passage, how would you define *abiding*?

5. **Read John 14:12.** What does Jesus mean when He promised that those who believe in Jesus will do greater works? (Hint: v. 12 most likely refers to greater in number rather than greater in quality.)

EXODUS 33:20 TEACHES THAT NO ONE CAN SEE GOD AND LIVE. THIS IS ONE REASON THE DISCIPLES WERE UNABLE TO UNDERSTAND HOW JESUS COULD REVEAL HIMSELF AS GOD.

JESUS' PROMISE

that He will do whatever is asked in His name appears **SEVEN TIMES** in the upcoming discourse

(JOHN 14:13, 14, 26; 15:16; 16:23, 24, 26).

Describe a time when you encountered a miraculous answer to prayer. (Note: If you're having a hard time thinking of a time remember . . . salvation, which is moving from death [the consequences of our sin] to eternal life by grace through faith in Jesus, is a miracle.)

6. **Read John 14:13–15.** Look up the following passages and fill in the chart below. Which of these passages inspires you to persist in prayer the most?

SCRIPTURE	WHAT THE PASSAGE REVEALS ABOUT PRAYER
Matthew 6:6–8	
Luke 11:9–13	
James 5:13–18	
1 John 5:14	

7. Prayer is not about getting large requests granted. It's about conforming our will to His will. God's will is more beautiful and farther reaching than a majority of our prayer requests. What's one bold, outrageous request (that you know is aligned with His will) you can make to Jesus now? Write it in the space below.

DAY 3
John 14:16–25

In the Upper Room, Jesus teaches on the power, presence, and person of the Holy Spirit.

1. **Read John 14:16–25.** What does Jesus call the Spirit (v. 17)?

How does the Spirit's title in verse 17 align with Jesus' title in John verse 6?

What does this reveal about the unity of Jesus and the Spirit?

THE GREEK WORD **PARAKLETOS**, REFERRING TO THE SPIRIT, CAN BE TRANSLATED **COMFORTER, ADVOCATE,** AND **COUNSELOR.**

2. **Reflecting on John 14:18,** describe a time when you have felt like an orphan.

How did Jesus meet you then?

3. **Reflecting on John 14:21,** what role does obedience have in loving and believing in Jesus?

On the continuum below, mark how obedient you are to Jesus.

I know I'm
disobeying
Jesus in
many ways.

I want to obey
Him more
than I do.

I'm fully, wholly
obedient to
Jesus in
every way.

4. Why is it important to do what Jesus commands rather than just study or know what Jesus commands?

5. What does Jesus promise to those who believe and obey Him in verses 21 and 23?

6. **Read John 14:25–31.** What are the specific ways in which the Holy Spirit brings comfort and help?

Which of these have you experienced?

Which of these do you want to experience more?

THROUGHOUT THE FINAL DISCOURSE Jesus TELLS THE DISCIPLES WHAT WILL HAPPEN SO THAT WHEN IT DOES, THEY WILL BELIEVE.

—JOHN 14:29

7. **Read John 15** to prepare for the next session. Summarize what happens in this chapter in two to three sentences.

What fills you with the most hope from this chapter?

How have you experienced Jesus as the True Vine?

reflection

As you reflect on your personal study of John 11–15, what are the BEAUTIFUL WORDS the Holy Spirit has been highlighting to you through this time? Write or draw them in the space below.

SESSION
7

I AM
THE VINE

John

opening group activity [10–15 MINUTES]

WHAT YOU'LL NEED:

Several kinds of grapes cut in clumps for tasting and sharing
Napkins

1. Invite participants to sample each type of grape and observe the textures, flavors, sizes, and how they're attached as a clump.

2. Discuss the following questions:

   Which is your favorite type of grape and why?

   What do you think Jesus was trying to communicate when He identified Himself as the Vine and declared "you are the branches" (John 15:5)?

   How connected to the Vine are you right now? What would help you become more connected?

   What's one question or topic from the homework or discussion that really challenged you or stuck with you?

watch session seven video [29 MINUTES]

Leader, play the streaming video or DVD.

As you watch, take notes while thinking through:

What caught your attention?
What surprised you?
What made you reflect?

The Gardener is the One who is in control.

 There's purpose to the pruning.

 Gardener is closest to the branches when He's pruning them.

 Branch doesn't tell Gardener what to do.

 Branches can't go it alone without the Vine.

 There are two ways to obey—duty and delight.

SCRIPTURE covered in this session:
John 15

group discussion questions (30-45 MINUTES)

Leader, read each numbered prompt and question to the group and select volunteers for Scripture reading.

1. **Read John 15:1, 5** aloud to the group. In Jesus' words, who is the Father? Who is Jesus? Who are you? Who is the source of life and control in this metaphor? Where do you struggle with trying to be in control? How does trying to be in control hinder or hurt your relationships with others? How does trusting the Father as Gardener free you? What would surrendering control and living in freedom look like practically?

2. **Read John 15:2.** On a scale of one to ten, how resistant are you to pruning in your life? Have you ever mistaken pruning for disfavor? If so, describe. When have you experienced pruning and found it yielded fruitfulness in your life?

3. How might God want to use your present pain to transform or conform or prune you into the likeness of Christ? What's easiest for you to accept about this? Hardest?

> "We're not the vine for others. We're not the source of life for others. Rather, we are to lead them to the True Vine." —Megan

4. Describe a time when you tried to be the source of life for someone instead of trusting Jesus. What was the result? When are you most tempted to take matters into your own hands and try to be the Gardener rather than the branch? How can you resist this temptation?

5. Select a volunteer to **read John 15:3–8** aloud to the group. What happens to a branch apart from the Vine? When have you tried to go it alone in your faith, life, or relationships? What was the fruit?

   How many times does the word *remain* appear in this passage?

   What does it look like for you to remain in Him (vv. 6–7)?

6. What is the difference between duty and delight when it comes to obedience to God? Where are you responding to God out of duty? Do you think it is bad to respond to God out of duty? Can feelings of delight arise as a result of duty-bound obedience? Where are you responding in obedience to God out of delight? Where are you most tempted in life to measure the outcomes rather than surrender the outcomes to God?

   How can you answer the call to abide in Christ this week? Write out a prayer asking God to help you abide in Him this week. You may need to ask Him to help you want to *want* to abide. You may choose to share your prayer with your group.

God is the Gardener, Jesus is the Vine, and we are the branches who abide.

close in prayer

Consider the following prompts as you pray together for:

- Greater trust in God as the source of power and control

- Willingness to submit to pruning

- Readiness to answer the call to abide in Christ

preparation

To prepare for the next group session:

1. **Read John 15–20.**

2. Tackle the three days of Session Seven Personal Study.

3. Memorize this week's passage using the Beautiful Word Scripture memory coloring page. As a bonus, look up the Scripture memory passage in different translations and take note of the variations.

4. If you've agreed to bring something for the next session's Opening Group Activity, get it ready.

"I am the vine; you are the branches. If you remain in me and I in you, you will bear much fruit; apart from me you can do nothing."
—John 15:5

PERSONAL
STUDY TIME

DIGGING INTO THE

Beautiful
WORD™
BIBLE STUDIES

John
I AM THE VINE

DAY 1
John 15–16

Jesus continues the conversation with the disciples in the Upper Room by identifying Himself as the True Vine and the Father as the Vinedresser. He then focuses on the relationships of the disciples with each other and the relationship of the disciples with the world.

1. **Read John 15:1–11.** What are promises to those who answer the call to abide in Christ in verses 7–11?

    Which of these do you need to experience in your life now? Why? What is your hope in this promise?

2. **Read John 13:34–35 and 15:12–17.** How does Jesus raise the standard of how we love one another?

3. How does it make you feel that God personally chose you? For what reason did He choose you (John 15:16)?

4. **Read John 15:18–27.** What reasons does Jesus give for the world's hatred?

5. Have you ever experienced hatred from the world because of your love of Christ? If so, describe.

6. **Read John 16:1–15.** What does Jesus reveal about the Holy Spirit?

Which of these have you personally experienced with the Holy Spirit?

7. **Read John 16:16–33.** Jesus echoes many of the teachings He's already given. What makes the difference in the disciples hearing and understanding? (Hint: vv. 25 and 29)

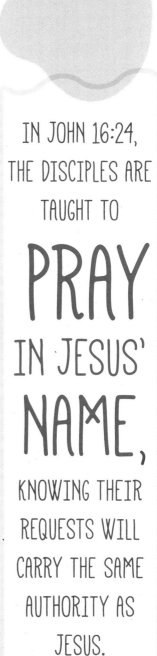

IN JOHN 16:24, THE DISCIPLES ARE TAUGHT TO PRAY IN JESUS' NAME, KNOWING THEIR REQUESTS WILL CARRY THE SAME AUTHORITY AS JESUS.

8. Which of Jesus' promises in this chapter is most meaningful to you now? Why?

DAY 2
John 17–18

Jesus takes time to pray for His disciples before His arrest. Sometimes called the "High Priestly Prayer," Jesus reveals His compassion and hope for the disciples and for us today.

1. **Read John 17:1–12.** What's the one request Jesus makes for Himself? (Hint: v. 1)

   How often do you think about God's glory in your prayers?

   If God were to say yes to the prayers you prayed this past week, would your life look more comfortable or would God be more glorified?

Why does Jesus ask His Holy Father to protect His disciples? (Hint: v. 11) Why is the reason for protection important?

2. **Read John 17:13–21.** How have you been sanctified or cleansed in the truth of Jesus?

How do you practice unity among fellow believers?

Take a moment and ask the Holy Spirit to bring to mind attitudes or actions that you need to stop or change to promote unity. Write what comes to mind below.

3. **Read John 17:22–26.** How has Jesus fulfilled His mission in verses 25–26?

SANCTIFICATION MEANS TO BE SET APART AND MADE HOLY, AND WE ARE SET APART BY THE TRUTH OF GOD'S WORD.

WHEN
JESUS
DECLARES IN JOHN 18:5,
"EGO EIMI"
WHICH MEANS
"I AM,"
THE FORCE OF
HIS WORDS
CAUSES EVERYONE
TO FALL BACKWARDS
TO THE GROUND.

....

....

....

....

....

....

....

....

....

....

In one to two sentences, write out your mission based on this passage.

Following Jesus' teaching and prayer, Jesus and the disciples go to the ravine of Kidron.

4. **Read John 18:1–11.** How do Judas and Peter respond to Jesus?

How does Jesus demonstrate His power with Judas, the soldiers, and Peter?

5. **Read John 13:37–38 and 18:12–27.** What causes Peter to make such a drastic change in His response to Christ?

What do Judas' and Peter's betrayals have in common? How are they different?

What situations and emotions tempt you to deny the realities of Christ in your life? Why is it you will never ultimately deny your Lord?

6. **Read John 18:28–40.** What stands out to you in the way Jesus responds to Pilate?

What stands out to you in the way Pilate responds to Jesus?

What does this reveal about Pilate's leadership and character?

DAY 3
John 19:1–20:29

The crowds are given a choice to set free Jesus, who brought truth and healing, or Barabbas, who brought falsities and robberies. The people choose Barabbas. What follows is the brutality, trauma, and the cruelty of the crucifixion.

1. **Read Isaiah 53:7 and John 19:1–15.** How does Jesus fulfill Isaiah's prophecy?

2. In this scene, how would you describe the attitudes of the following:

Jesus:

Pilate:

The soldiers:

The Jews:

"THEREFORE I WILL GIVE HIM A PORTION AMONG THE GREAT, AND HE WILL DIVIDE THE SPOILS WITH THE STRONG, BECAUSE HE POURED OUT HIS LIFE UNTO DEATH, AND WAS NUMBERED WITH THE TRANSGRESSORS. FOR HE BORE THE SIN OF MANY, AND MADE INTERCESSION FOR THE TRANSGRESSORS."

— ISAIAH 53:12

3. Before you continue reading Jesus' journey to the cross, **read Romans 5:8 and Romans 6:23**. Why did Jesus die?

4. **Read John 19:16–30 slowly.** Write down at least three observations that stood out to you as you read it.

- _____
  _____
  _____

- _____
  _____
  _____
  _____

- _____
  _____
  _____

A TEACHER WAS ONCE ASKED, "WHAT IS MORE IMPORTANT IN PRAYER, SPEAKING TO GOD OR LISTENING TO GOD?"

HE ANSWERED: "WHAT IS MORE IMPORTANT TO YOUR LIFE, BREATHING OUT OR BREATHING IN?"

5. What were the last words of Jesus that John records (v. 30)? What do you think His words mean?

6. **Read John 19:31–42.** Following Jesus' death, would your response have been more like the disciples, Nicodemus, or Joseph of Arimathea? Why?

7. **Read John 20–21** to prepare for the next session. Summarize what happens in these chapters in two to three sentences.

What fills you with the most hope from these chapters?

What do you love most about how the Gospel of John concludes?

reflection

As you reflect on your personal study of John 15–21, what are the BEAUTIFUL WORDS the Holy Spirit has been highlighting to you through this time? Write or draw them in the space below.

SESSION 8

FIND LIFE
IN HIS NAME

John

opening group activity [10–15 MINUTES]

WHAT YOU'LL NEED:

Each person to bring food to share

Party balloons or fun decorations

1. Decorate the room with balloons, streamers, wildflowers, and anything you can find to create a festive atmosphere.

2. Enjoy laughing, talking, sharing, and catching up as you eat together.

3. Discuss the following questions:

   What have you enjoyed most about the Gospel of John?

   What's one question or topic from the homework or discussion that really challenged you or stuck with you?

watch session eight video [32 MINUTES]

Leader, play the streaming video or DVD.

As you watch, take notes while thinking through::

What caught your attention?
What surprised you?
What made you reflect?

❋ I plead Jesus, not myself.

❋ Jesus perfectly models how to live with the end in mind.

❋ The light of men—torches, lanterns—cannot stand before the light of God.

❋ Every act surrounding Jesus' death is a testimony of God's love and sacrifice.

❋ Propitiation means averting the wrath of God through the offering of a gift.

❋ Belief transforms life daily and eternally.

SCRIPTURE covered in this session:
John 20–21

group discussion questions [30–45 MINUTES]

Leader, read each numbered prompt and question to the group and select volunteers for Scripture reading.

1. If you knew you had one week to live, would you live exactly as you had this past week? How does thinking about the end of your life and eternity affect the way you live now? Your present trials?

> "Imagine the day you will stand before God. We all will, right? What will He ask you? Do you love Me? Do you believe in Me? And did your life demonstrate it? Did you learn to love?" —Megan

2. How would you answer each of these questions? What changes do you need to make to live a more God-centric life?

3. **Select volunteers to read John 20:1–18 aloud to the group.** Who are the three witnesses to the empty tomb? What stands out to you most about the interaction between Jesus and Mary? What does it say about Jesus' perspective on women that He would see her first after the resurrection and then send her out to tell the disciples (v. 18)?

   Why is the resurrection so important? How would Christianity and your life be different if there was no resurrection?

"**B**elief is not simply knowing. We can collect knowledge about something—chairs are sturdy, made of wood, you can sit in them, and they will hold your weight. Then we can agree with something—I believe this chair would hold me if I sat in it. And then there is trust in it—I am going to actually sit down in this chair because I trust and believe it to hold me." —Megan

4. Reflecting on your faith journey, which of the following best describes you—collecting knowledge about Jesus, agreeing with the teachings of Jesus, or trusting and believing in Jesus?

5. True trust (saving faith) necessarily involves action; it is not mere assent. You can only find rest in a chair when you actually take a seat in it. Putting your weight in something involves risk. By putting your weight in the chair you are risking that it will not hold you. But by truly trusting in Jesus you are wagering your eternity on the faith that He is whom He says He is. Reflecting on the seven *I Am* statements of Jesus, which is the easiest, like a chair, to place all your weight on, and believe? Which is the hardest, like a chair, to place all your weight on, and believe?

6. Select volunteers to **read John 21:15–19** aloud. How does Jesus restore Peter after his triple denial? What's one area where Jesus has restored you? Where in your life do you long for Jesus to restore you?

7. **Read John 20:31** aloud. How have you experienced this through your reading of the Gospel of John? How would you sum up Jesus' *I Am* statements in a few words?

What's your biggest takeaway from this Beautiful Word study?

How may the Holy Spirit be empowering you to live differently because of this discovery?

The fruit of your life is the evidence of your belief in Jesus.

close in prayer

Consider the following prompts as you pray together for:

- Deeper belief and trust in Jesus in every area of life

- Renewed desire to live a God-centric life

- Readiness to follow and proclaim Jesus wherever He leads

preparation

To conclude:

1. Tackle the three days of Session Eight Personal Study.

2. Memorize this week's passage using the Beautiful Word Scripture memory coloring page. As a bonus, look up the Scripture memory passage in different translations and take note of the variations.

"Follow me!"

—John 21:19

PERSONAL STUDY TIME

DIGGING INTO THE

Beautiful
WORD™
BIBLE STUDIES

John

FIND LIFE IN HIS NAME

DAY 1
John 20:1–21:11

After the brutal crucifixion, the Gospel of John states that Mary Magdalene goes to the tomb and makes a startling discovery.

1. **Read John 20:1–28.** Who believes Jesus has been resurrected in this passage?

How do their stories of belief differ?

What do they have in common?

To whom do you relate best when it comes to your own journey of belief? Why?

2. **Read John 20:29–31.** What is the writer of the Gospel of John's goal?

Do you think the author met this goal? Why or why not?

Do you think the author met this goal with you personally? Why or why not?

3. **Read John 21:1–6 and Luke 5:1–6.** What parallels do you see between these two passages?

Why do you suspect Jesus performed this miracle multiple times?

IN JOHN 20:1–2, **MARY MAGDALENE** IS NOTED AS BEING THE FIRST TO THE TOMB AND SEEING THE STONE ROLLED AWAY, BUT IN VERSE 2, SHE SAYS **"WE DON'T KNOW"** IMPLYING OTHERS WERE WITH HER.

4. **Read John 21:7.** How does Peter respond to the news that Jesus is on the shore?

How does this compare with Peter denying Jesus three times? How does this compare with the reaction of Judas?

When you make a mistake do you tend to run toward Jesus or hide in the shadows?

5. On the continuum below, mark which you tend to focus on more.

①← ② — ③ — ④ — ⑤ — ⑥ — ⑦ — ⑧ — ⑨ → ⑩

I tend to focus
on my failures.

I tend to focus
on God's
forgiveness.

How does what you focus on affect your ability to move forward?

6. Is there an area of your life where you feel trapped in sin?

How can you allow Christ's forgiveness to set you free?

7. **Read John 21:4–13.** Why do you think the disciples recognized Jesus in verse 12 after not recognizing Him in verse 4?

What does verse 13 remind you of?

DAY 2
John 21:12-21

After a miraculous catch, Jesus spends time sharing a meal with the disciples.

1. **Read John 21:15–17.** To what lengths does Jesus go to show His love, forgiveness, and restoration power to Peter?

   To what lengths do you believe Jesus will go (or perhaps has already gone) to love, forgive, and restore you?

2. How does Jesus restore Peter?

   How do you respond to your failures?

   What do we learn about the heart of God from this passage in how He responds to Peter's failures? In light of this, how do you think Jesus views your own failures? How does Jesus' view of your failures differ from how you see your failures?

3. Reflecting on Jesus' response to Peter, how are the love of Christ and service to others intertwined?

4. **Read John 21:18–25.** How does Peter get distracted by what Jesus says to another disciple?

5. It's been said that comparison is the thief of all joy. When are you most tempted to get distracted or fall into the comparison trap with others?

6. How has your understanding and belief in the life, death, and resurrection of Jesus changed through this Beautiful Word study?

DAY 3
Your Beautiful Word

Review your notes and responses throughout this study guide. Place a star by those that stand out to you. Then respond to the following questions.

1. What are three of the most important truths you learned from studying the *I Am* statements in John? How have those truths set you free?

2. After reviewing the eight Beautiful Word coloring pages, which *I Am* statement stands out to you the most? Why?

3. What's one practical application from studying the *I Am* statements that you've put into practice? What's one practical application from the study that you would still like to put into practice?

4. How has the Holy Spirit prompted changes in your attitudes, actions, and behaviors as a result of studying the *I Am* statements?

5. How has the Holy Spirit produced even more fruit in your life as you've abided in the True Vine?

6. How can you worship God in Spirit and in truth (worshipping God with all that you are in response to the truth of whom He is) in response to His work in your life through this study?

reflection

As you reflect on your personal study and John 20–21, what are the BEAUTIFUL WORDS that the Holy Spirit has been highlighting to you personally through this time? Write or draw them in the space below.

SMALL GROUP LEADER'S GUIDE

If you are reading this, you have likely agreed to lead a group through *John: Believe I Am*. Thank you! What you have chosen to do is important, and much good fruit can come from studies like this. The rewards of being a leader are different from those participating, and we hope you find your own walk with Jesus deepened by this experience.

John is an eight-session study built around video content and small-group interaction. As the group leader, imagine yourself as the host of a dinner party. Your job is to take care of your guests by managing all the behind-the-scenes details so that as your guests arrive, they can focus on each other and on interaction around the topic.

As the group leader, your role is NOT to answer all the questions or reteach the content—the video, book, and study guide will do most of that work. Your job is to guide the experience and cultivate your small group into a kind of welcoming, teaching community. This will make it a place for members to process, question, reflect, and grow—not receive more instruction.

There are several elements in this leader's guide that will help you as you structure your study and reflection time, so follow along and take advantage of each one.

BEFORE YOU BEGIN

MATERIALS

Before your first meeting, make sure the participants have a copy of this study guide so they can follow along and have their answers written out ahead of time. Alternately, you can hand out the study guides at your first meeting and give the group members some time to look over the material and ask any preliminary questions. During your first meeting, be sure to send a sheet around the room and have the members write down their names, phone numbers, and email addresses so you can keep in touch with them during the week.

VIDEO STREAMING ACCESS

Additionally, spend a few minutes going over how to access the streaming video using the instructions printed in each study guide. Helping everyone understand how accessible this material is will go a long way if anyone (including you) has to miss a meeting or if a member of your group chooses to lead a study after the conclusion of this one!

A few commonly-asked questions and answers:

Do I have to subscribe to StudyGateway? NO. If you sign up for StudyGateway for the first time using StudyGateway.com/Redeem, you will not be prompted to pay for a subscription during the code redemption process.

Do I set up another account if I do another study later? NO. The next time you do a HarperChristian Resources study with streaming access, all you need to do is enter the new access code and the videos will be added to your account library.

There is a short video available, walking you through how to access your streaming videos. You can choose to show the video at your first meeting, or simply direct your group to the HarperChristian Resources YouTube channel to watch it at their convenience.

GROUP SIZE

Generally, the ideal size for a group is between eight to ten people, which ensures everyone will have enough time to participate in discussions. If you have more people, you might want to break up the main group into smaller subgroups. Encourage those who show up at the first meeting to commit to attending the duration of the study, as this will help the group members get to know each other, create stability for the group, and help you know how to prepare each week.

OPENING ACTIVITY

Each of the sessions begins with an opening activity, which you, the leader, should read through and practice prior to your group meeting if it seems new to you.

There are a few questions that follow the activity which serve as an icebreaker to get the group members thinking about the topic for the week. Some people may want to tell a long story in response to one of these questions, but the goal is to keep the answers brief. Ideally, you want everyone in the group to get a chance to answer, so try to keep the responses to a minute or less. If you have talkative group members, say up front that everyone needs to limit his or her answer to one minute.

Give the group members a chance to answer but tell them to feel free to pass if they wish. With the rest of the study, it's generally not a good idea to have everyone answer every question—a free-flowing discussion is more desirable. But with the opening icebreaker questions, you can go around the circle. Encourage shy people to share, but don't force them.

PREPARING YOUR GROUP FOR THE STUDY

Before watching your first video at your first meeting, let the group members know that each session contains three days' worth of Bible study and reflection materials to complete during the week. While the personal study is optional, it will help the members cement the concepts presented during the group study time and encourage them to spend time each day in God's Word. The *Beautiful Word Bible Studies* series is designed so each participant reads through the entire book of the Bible being studied over the course of the personal study exercises. One of the most commonly-lamented aspects of all church ministry is struggling to get people to read their Bibles on their own. We have made reading a book of the Bible as simple and engaging as ever and your group members will not believe what they get out of spending time each week engaging God's Word for themselves!

Also, invite your group members to bring any questions and insights they uncovered while reading to your next meeting, especially if they had a breakthrough moment or if they didn't understand something.

WEEKLY PREPARATION

As the leader, there are a few things you should do to prepare for each meeting:

- *Watch the video.* This will help you to become familiar with the content Megan is presenting and give you foresight of what may or may not be brought up in the discussion time.

- *Read through the group discussion section.* This will help you to become familiar with the questions you will be asking and allow you to better determine how to structure the discussion time for your particular group.

- *Decide which questions you definitely want to discuss.* Based on the amount and length of group discussion, you may not be able to get through all the questions, so choose four to five questions that you definitely want to cover.

- *Be familiar with the questions you want to discuss.* Every group has times when there are no respondents and the question falls flat out of the gate. This is normal and okay! Be prepared with YOUR answer to the questions so you can always offer to share as an icebreaker and example. What you want to avoid is always answering the questions and therefore speaking for the group. Foremost, encourage members of the group to answer questions.

- *Remind your group there are no wrong answers or dumb questions.* Note that in many cases there will be no one "right" answer to the question. Answers will vary, especially when the group members are being asked to share their personal experiences.

- *Pray for your group.* Pray for your group members throughout the week and ask God to lead them as they study His Word.

- *Bring extra supplies to your meeting.* The members should bring their own pens for writing notes, but it's a good idea to have extras available for those who forget. You may also want to bring paper and additional Bibles.

STRUCTURING THE DISCUSSION TIME

You will need to determine with your group how long you want to meet each week so you can plan your time accordingly. Generally, most groups like to meet for either sixty minutes or ninety minutes, so you could use one of the following schedules:

SECTION	60 MINUTES	90 MINUTES
INTRODUCTION (Members arrive and get settled; leader reads or summarizes the introduction.)	5 minutes	10 minutes
OPENING ACTIVITY	10 minutes	15 minutes
VIDEO NOTES (Watch the teaching video together and take notes.)	15 minutes	15 minutes
GROUP DISCUSSION (Discuss the Bible study questions you selected ahead of time.)	25 minutes	40 minutes
CLOSING PRAYER (Pray together as a group and dismiss.)	5 minutes	10 minutes

As the group leader, it is up to you to keep track of the time and keep things moving along according to your schedule. You might want to set a timer for each segment so both you and the group members know when your time is up. (Note: There are some good phone apps for timers that play a gentle chime or other pleasant sound instead of a disruptive noise.)

Don't be concerned if the group members are quiet or slow to share. People are often quiet when they are pulling together their ideas, and this might be a new experience for them. Just ask a question and let it hang in the air until someone shares. You can then say, "Thank you. What about others? What came to you when you watched that portion of the video?"

GROUP DYNAMICS

Leading a group through *John* will prove to be highly rewarding both for you and your group members. However, this doesn't mean you will not encounter any challenges along the way! Discussions can get off track. Group members may not be sensitive to the needs and ideas of others. Some might worry they will be expected to talk about matters that make them feel awkward. Others may express comments that result in disagreements. To help ease this strain on you and the group, consider the following ground rules:

- When someone raises a question or comment that is off the main topic, suggest you deal with it another time, or, if you feel led to go in that direction, let the group know you will be spending some time discussing it.

- If someone asks a question you don't know how to answer, admit it and move on. At your discretion, feel free to invite group members to comment on questions that call for personal experience.

- If you find one or two people are dominating the discussion time, direct a few questions to others in the group. Outside the main group time, ask the more dominating members to help you draw out the quieter ones. Work to make them a part of the solution instead of the problem.

- When a disagreement occurs, encourage the group members to process the matter in love. Encourage those on opposite sides to restate what they heard the other side say about the matter, and then invite each side to evaluate if that perception is accurate. Lead the group in examining other Scriptures related to the topic and look for common ground.

When any of these issues arise, encourage your group members to follow these words from the Bible: "Love one another" (John 13:34), "If it is possible, as far as it depends on you, live at peace with everyone" (Romans 12:18), and "Be quick to listen, slow to speak and slow to become angry" (James 1:19). This will make your group time more rewarding and beneficial for everyone who attends.

SESSION BY SESSION OVERVIEWS

SESSION 1: BELIEVE I AM

Scripture covered in this session: **John 1:1–5, 14**

Scripture to study and read this week: **John chapters 1–6**

Verse of the Week: "But these are written that you may believe that Jesus is the Messiah, the Son of God, and that by believing you may have life in his name" (John 20:31).

Discussion Question choices / notes:

PRAYER REQUESTS

SESSION 2: I AM THE BREAD OF LIFE

Scripture covered in this session: **John 6**

Scripture to study and read this week: **John chapters 6–8**

Verse of the Week: "I am the bread of life. Whoever comes to me will never go hungry, and whoever believes in me will never be thirsty" (John 6:35).

Discussion Question choices / notes:

PRAYER REQUESTS

SESSION 3: I AM THE LIGHT OF THE WORLD

Scripture covered in this session: **John 8**

Scripture to read this week: **John chapters 8–10**

Verse of the Week: "I am the light of the world. Whoever follows me will never walk in darkness, but will have the light of life" (John 8:12).

Discussion Question choices / notes:

PRAYER REQUESTS

SESSION 4: I AM THE GATE AND THE GOOD SHEPHERD

Scripture covered in this session: **John 10**

Scripture to read this week: **John chapters 10–11**

Verse of the Week: "Very truly I tell you, I am the gate for the sheep … I am the good shepherd. The good shepherd lays down his life for the sheep" (John 10:7, 11).

Discussion Question choices / notes:

PRAYER REQUESTS

SESSION 5: I AM THE RESURRECTION AND THE LIFE

Scripture covered in this session: **John 11**

Scripture to study and read this week: **John chapters 11–14**

Verse of the Week: "I am the resurrection and the life. The one who believes in me will live, even though they die" (John 11:25).

Discussion Question choices / notes:

PRAYER REQUESTS

SESSION 6: I AM THE WAY, THE TRUTH, AND THE LIFE

Scripture covered in this session: **John 14**

Scripture to study and read this week: **John chapters 14–15**

Verse of the Week: "I am the way and the truth and the life. No one comes to the Father except through me" (John 14:6).

Discussion Question choices / notes:

PRAYER REQUESTS

SESSION 7: I AM THE VINE

Scripture covered in this session: **John 15**
Scripture to study and read this week: **John chapters 15–20**

Verse of the Week: "I am the vine; you are the branches. If you remain in me and I in you, you will bear much fruit; apart from me you can do nothing" (John 15:5).

Discussion Question choices / notes:

PRAYER REQUESTS

SESSION EIGHT: FIND LIFE IN HIS NAME

Scripture covered in this session: **John 20**
Scripture to study and read this week: **John chapters 20–21**

Verse of the Week: "Follow me!" (John 21:19).

Discussion Question choices / notes:

PRAYER REQUESTS

SCRIPTURE MEMORY CARDS

SESSION 1

"But these are written that you may believe that Jesus is the Messiah, the Son of God, and that by believing you may have life in his name."

—John 20:31

SESSION 2

"I am the bread of life. Whoever comes to me will never go hungry, and whoever believes in me will never be thirsty."

—John 6:35

SESSION 3

"I am the light of the world. Whoever follows me will never walk in darkness, but will have the light of life."

—John 8:12

SESSION 4

"Very truly I tell you, I am the gate for the sheep . . . I am the good shepherd. The good shepherd lays down his life for the sheep."

—John 10:7, 11

SCRIPTURE MEMORY CARDS

SESSION 5

"I am the resurrection and the life. The one who believes in me will live, even though they die."

—John 11:25

SESSION 6

"I am the way and the truth and the life. No one comes to the Father except through me."

—John 14:6

SESSION 7

"I am the vine; you are the branches. If you remain in me and I in you, you will bear much fruit; apart from me you can do nothing."

—John 15:5

SESSION 8

"Follow me!"

—John 21:19

ABOUT THE AUTHOR

Megan Fate Marshman is an international speaker at churches, conferences, and university chapels. She is a leading voice to this generation. She has devoted her life to loving God and overflowing His awesome love to others.

Megan is finishing her Doctorate in Ministry as she serves as a teaching pastor at Willow Creek Community Church and the Director of Women's Ministries at Hume Lake Christian Camps. She also shepherds women at Arbor Road Church. She enjoys adventuring all over the globe with her boys, sharing the love of Jesus.

Megan lives in Lakewood, California, with her two boys, Foster and Jedidiah. www.meganfate .com.

In this six-session video Bible study, Megan Fate Marshman will take you through an engaging exploration of the significance of Jeremiah 29:11–14. Through interactive Bible study exercises, you will discover how to stop discounting yourself from a hopeful future, start living in active dependence on God, how to trust God's definition of good above your own.

Discover the Beauty of God's Word

The Beautiful Word™ Bible Study Series helps you connect God's Word to your daily life through vibrant video teaching, group discussion, and deep personal study that includes verse-by-verse reading, Scripture memory, coloring pages, and encouragement to receive your own beautiful Word from God.

In each study, a central theme—a beautiful word—threads throughout the book, helps you connect and apply each book of the Bible to your daily life today, and forever.

IN THIS SERIES:

GALATIANS — Jada Edwards — Available Now
REVELATION — Margaret Feinberg — Available Now
EPHESIANS — Lori Wilhite — Available Now
ROMANS — Jada Edwards — Available Now
PHILIPPIANS — Lori Wilhite — Available Now
JOHN — Megan Fate Marshman — Fall 2022
LUKE — Lisa Harper — Spring 2023

Study Guide

Study Guide with Streaming Video

Study Guide

Study Guide with Streaming Video

These Bible studies, along with Beautiful Word™ Bibles and Bible Journals are available wherever books are sold. Streaming video available on StudyGateway.com.